BARACK OBAMA
OUR 44TH PRESIDENT

By Beatrice Gormley

SCHOLASTIC INC.

New York Toronto London Auckland
Sydney New Delhi Hong Kong

To my husband, Bob

Cover: Getty Images.

Design by Lisa Vega.
The text of this book was set in Cochin.

Copyright © 2008 by Beatrice Gormley.
All rights reserved.
Published by Scholastic Inc.,
557 Broadway, New York, NY 10012,
by arrangement with Simon & Schuster Children's Publishing Division.
Printed in the U.S.A.

ISBN-13: 978-0-545-21841-2
ISBN-10: 0-545-21841-1

1 2 3 4 5 6 7 8 9 10   40   18 17 16 15 14 13 12 11 10 09

BARACK OBAMA
OUR
44TH PRESIDENT

Contents

BARACK OBAMA
OUR
44TH PRESIDENT

Chapter 1

Barack Obama, Jr.

On August 4, 1961, a baby boy was born at Kapi'olani Medical Center in Honolulu, Hawaii. He weighed eight pounds, two ounces. His parents, Ann and Barack, named him after his father, Barack Hussein Obama, but they called their child "Barry."

Barack Obama, Sr., was a foreign exchange student from Kenya, a country in east-central Africa. He was twenty-five years old, studying on a scholarship at the University of Hawaii. He was the very first African student at the school.

Barack was tall and charming, with a voice "like black velvet," as his mother-in-law Madelyn Dunham described it, "with a British accent." He had come from a poor family, herding goats as a boy. His father, of the Luo tribe, had been a domestic servant for the

British colonials. Now Kenya was on the brink of gaining independence from Britain.

Barack was determined to accomplish great things, both for himself and for his country. It was a great honor for a youth from his humble background to study at American schools and earn an advanced degree in economics. But he also had a heavy responsibility to his people, and he intended to return to Kenya and help lead the country into a brighter future.

Ann Dunham was an eighteen-year-old freshman at the University of Hawaii in 1960 when she met Barack in a Russian class. A quiet but independent-minded girl, she had dark curly hair and dark eyebrows like her father's. She read serious books about reforming society, and she eagerly spent hours in long, earnest discussions with her friends.

Ann lived with her parents, Stanley and Madelyn Dunham, in a rambling house near the university campus. Stanley was a furniture salesman, while Madelyn worked for a bank. Both Stanley and Madelyn had grown up in Kansas, but after they married, they lived in several states before settling in Hawaii.

When Ann first brought Barack home for dinner, her parents, especially Madelyn, were uneasy. They had never met anyone from Africa before. But Barack quickly won them over with his charm, and they were impressed with his brilliant mind and his confidence.

However, the Dunhams were unpleasantly surprised in February 1961, when Ann and Barack eloped to the island of Maui and came back married. Stanley and Madelyn were disappointed that Ann, so bright and inquisitive of mind, was dropping out of college after only one semester. Madelyn also feared that the cultural differences between their American daughter and this African young man were too great.

Barack's father, Hussein Onyango Obama, who lived in Kenya, was also surprised and very upset at the news. He threatened to get Barack's travel visa cancelled, so he'd have to return to Kenya. He pointed out that Barack already had family responsibilities: a wife and two children in Kenya. Also, he warned his son, an American wife wasn't likely to be understanding about the African custom of a man having more than one family. Furthermore, Onyango wrote Stanley Dunham a long, angry letter. As Barry's mother told him years later, Barack's father "didn't want the Obama blood sullied by a white woman."

Barack refused to obey his father, and the Dunhams accepted their daughter's choice. For two years Barack and Ann lived with their baby in a small white house near the university campus. Then in 1963, Barack graduated from the University of Hawaii and won a scholarship to study economics at Harvard University in Massachusetts. The scholarship didn't allow enough money to bring Ann and their son with him, but Barack felt he couldn't pass up the chance to study at such a prestigious university. In the end, he left Hawaii for Massachusetts by himself.

Barack, Sr., intended to eventually take his wife and son back to Kenya, after he had earned his PhD in economics. But Ann decided that this marriage would not work. Barack might love her and Barry, but his wife and son were not as important as his fierce ambition or his commitment to Kenya. Besides, it did matter to Ann, as Barack's father had predicted, that Barack had a wife and children in Kenya. In January 1964, she filed for divorce.

During his first years, Barry didn't wonder why his father was missing. Family pictures show him happily riding his tricycle or perched on a fence with his mother's arm around him. In another picture from those days, Barry frolics in the surf with his grandfather Stanley (whom Barry called "Gramps"). A boisterous, outgoing man, Stanley was delighted to have Barry to play with and show off to friends and neighbors. Madelyn Dunham was more practical and sensible, but she too doted on their grandson. She told him to call her "Tutu," Hawaiian for "grandmother," and the name got shortened to "Toot."

Barry's mother and grandparents talked to him about his father, but they never criticized Barack, Sr., to Barry. Ann especially must have felt pain and anger over the failed marriage, but she didn't say anything to Barry about that. The worst thing she said about Barack Obama was that he was a terrible driver.

Ann told Barry that he had a wonderful father — fiercely intelligent, with a deep baritone voice and a way of commanding people's attention. She showed him pictures of Barack, Sr., a dark-skinned man with glasses. She told him his father loved him very much.

Although Barry wouldn't realize it for many years, his mother was just as remarkable as his father. Her full name was Stanley Ann Dunham, because her father had wished for a son. Growing up, she didn't like having a boy's name, but feeling different from other children may have made her more independent as well.

Once, when the Dunhams were living in Texas, Ann brought a black friend home to play. That would have been fine with Ann's parents, but the neighborhood children taunted the girls with racial slurs, driving the black girl away. Even more disturbing, the adult townspeople blamed the incident on the Dunhams. Instead of scolding their own children, they advised the Dunhams not to let Ann associate with black playmates.

When Ann was in the eighth grade, the family moved to Seattle, Washington. Stanley was offered a better job in a furniture store there, and they were all glad to leave Texas. Madelyn found a job in a bank. In 1956, the Dunhams bought a house on Mercer Island, near Seattle, so that Ann could attend the new high school there.

Ann was an idealistic and curious girl, with a mind of her own. Some of her high school friends were surprised that she didn't feel any need to fit in with other young people. She didn't seem to have the usual interest in dating or eventually getting married and having children.

What did interest Ann were current events and the controversial ideas set forth by her English and philosophy teachers. These teachers angered many in the community by questioning religion, the U.S. political system, and other parts of the American way of life. Some of the thought-provoking books they assigned were Vance Packard's *The Hidden Persuaders*, about the power of advertising; George Orwell's *1984*, a novel about a grim future in which the countries of the world are always at war and the government controls citizens' minds with lies and violence; and William Whyte's *The Organization Man*, which described big American corporations as controlling every aspect of their employees' lives.

Ann and her friends had long discussions on such topics after school in coffee shops. She spent much of her free time reading. She was fascinated with other cultures, and she was idealistic about how people's lives could be improved.

Toward the end of her high school career, Ann applied to the University of Chicago and received early acceptance. The University of Chicago, with its reputation for intellectual excitement, in the middle of a big city, appealed to Ann's sense of adventure. However, Stanley Dunham didn't want his daughter living on her own, far away from home, at such a young age.

After Ann's graduation from high school, in 1960, Stanley heard that a new opportunity was opening up in the furniture business in Honolulu. Always ready for a new adventure and hopeful for a better life somewhere else, he decided to move the family to Hawaii.

Ann resented her father for running her life, and she was reluctant to leave Seattle. But Hawaii wasn't such a bad place to be: a land of warm, sandy beaches and transparent blue water, of steep rain-forest-covered hills with waterfalls and ginger flow-ers. Also, in Hawaii Ann encountered people with an interesting mix of backgrounds: Japanese, Fili-pino, Polynesian. Ann enrolled in the University of Hawaii to study anthropology. She soon fell in with a group of students who shared her interest in poli-tics and world affairs. One of them—the one with the most forceful, confident opinions—was Barack Obama.

After divorcing Barack in 1964, Ann went back to school at the University of Hawaii. She had no money, but she got by with food stamps and with her parents' help. While Ann was in class, Barry's grandparents took care of him.

Ann soon met another foreign exchange student she liked very much, an Indonesian man named Lolo Soetoro. Indonesia, like Kenya, was a recently indepen-dent country. Lolo's father and brother had both died in the struggle against the Dutch colonialists, and the Dutch army had burned their house. Lolo was proud of his country and wanted to contribute to building a better Indonesia. He planned to teach at the university when he returned to Jakarta, the capital city.

Having a much more easygoing personality than Barack, Sr., Lolo got along well with the Dunhams. He enjoyed tussling with young Barry and playing chess with Stanley. Lolo wanted to remain in Hawaii until he finished his studies, but Indonesia in the mid-1960s was a country in turmoil.

President Sukarno had ruled Indonesia since the declaration of independence in 1945, but there was increasing unrest against his government. In 1965 the army led a violent anti-communist purge in which hundreds of thousands died. In 1966, Lolo was ordered back to Indonesia to serve in the army. He and Ann decided to marry before he left, with the plan that she and Barry would join him several months later.

Stanley was excited for Ann and Barry, moving to a place more exotic than Hawaii, with tigers and monsoons. Madelyn was worried that the country might not be safe for them, because of the political upheaval. Ann and Barry needed to get shots and passports, since they'd never left the United States before. In 1967 they boarded a plane to fly first to Japan and then to Jakarta, Indonesia, about a third of the way around the globe from Hawaii.

Chapter 2

Indonesia

Both Hawaii and Indonesia are tropical archipelagoes, or chains of islands, but there the resemblance ends. Indonesia, including the principal islands of Java, Borneo, Sumatra, and Bali, is a hundred times greater in land area than Hawaii. At the time Barry and his family lived in Indonesia, its population was well over 100 million, while Hawaii's population was around 700,000. Even the weather is different. In Honolulu, although the temperature is usually very warm, the constant trade winds make it feel comfortable. Jakarta, lying right near the equator, is extremely hot and steamy.

Six-year-old Barry Obama and his mother were thrilled with the adventure of living in an entirely strange place. As Lolo drove them home from the airport the first day, he pointed out a towering statue of Hanuman the monkey god. At Lolo's house Barry found baby crocodiles in the backyard, as well as an ape, specially bought as a pet for Barry. Birds of paradise, trailing extravagant plumage, perched in the trees. There were also chickens in the backyard—and one of them, Barry was astounded to learn, would be slaughtered for their dinner.

The Indonesian language was incomprehensible to Barry at first, and he didn't know anyone except his mother and stepfather. However, Lolo's relatives were warm and welcoming to his American wife and stepson. In the neighborhood, Barry set out to make friends. Perching on the garden wall, he flapped his arms and cawed like a crow to make the other children laugh.

Soon Barry was kicking a soccer ball around with the other children. There was no end of exciting things to do: playing in rice paddies, riding on water buffalo, flying kites in fierce contests. He learned to eat unfamiliar things like tofu and tempeh, spiced with hot peppers. He learned to expect the teachers at his new school to lash him with a bamboo switch if he misbehaved. Lolo, a caring stepfather, taught Barry how to defend himself if another boy picked a fight.

One of the strangest things about Indonesia,

for both Ann and Barry, was the poverty. Although Lolo's house had no electricity, it was a comfortable white stucco house with a red tiled roof. But many of their neighbors lived in bamboo huts. The neighboring farmers might lose their whole year's crop if there was a drought, and they were helpless against severe floods.

And then there were hordes of beggars: homeless, jobless, orphaned, blind, deformed, or with hideous diseases like leprosy. Ann was so tenderhearted that her eyes filled with tears and her chin trembled at the sight of these truly destitute people. She wanted to help everyone who came to the door and asked for money.

But Lolo had a different attitude. He told Barry that life was hard, and that was just the way it was. He gave hints about what *he* had endured the year that General Suharto's government yanked him away from his studies in Hawaii and sent him into the swamps of New Guinea to fight the communist rebels. He showed Barry the scars on his legs where he'd dug leeches out with a hot knife.

It was impractical, Lolo explained, to try to help everyone who needed help. It was hard enough just to take care of yourself and your family. Lolo was lucky to be educated and have a job, working for the army as a geologist. He intended to get a better job and move up in the world.

Lolo was Muslim, although not very devout. He sometimes went to the mosque to pray, and once in a long while he took Barry with him. Islam, as many Indonesians practiced it, included elements of Hinduism, such as the monkey god Hanuman, as well as bits of the religion of the original Indonesian tribes. Everyone in Lolo's neighborhood was Muslim, but Ann and Lolo sent Barry to a Catholic school, Franciscus Assisi Primary School. All the children there, including Barry, were expected to take part in the daily Catholic prayers, although it was merely a rote exercise to Barry.

At school, as in his neighborhood, Barry didn't see anyone who looked like him. This was different from Hawaii, where the population was a mix of various ethnic groups: the Polynesians who first settled the islands, the white Europeans who arrived in the eighteenth century, the Asians who began immigrating there in the nineteenth century, and many other groups who'd arrived since. Here all the children were short, slight Indonesians—except for tall, husky Barry. His skin was darker than theirs, and his hair was curly rather than straight.

Barry had to work to learn the new language, and he was sometimes teased for being a foreigner and different looking. Once a friend tricked him into eating a piece of shrimp paste, telling him it was chocolate. At least Barry knew the Indonesian word for this situation. *"Curang, curang!"* he shouted at the other boy, spitting out the shrimp paste. "Cheater, cheater!"

But Barry, a cheerful and outgoing boy, wasn't discouraged by the teasing. He was naturally kind, protecting smaller children and helping up anyone who fell down. His first-grade teacher, Israella Darmawan, noticed how bright he was, and how the other children tended to follow his lead.

Meanwhile, Ann took a job as an English teacher at the U.S. embassy in Jakarta. She was already tutoring Barry in English, waking him up early to study before school every morning. While Ann wanted Barry to adapt to Indonesia, she didn't want him to lose ground in his native language.

In 1970, Ann gave birth to a daughter, Maya Kassandra Soetoro. She taught Maya from an early age, as she had Barry, that everyone was the same under the skin. All people had the right to be respected. Maya's doll collection looked "like the United Nations," as she said later. There was a black doll, an Inuit doll, a Dutch doll.

Barry's mother coached him to be proud of his own special identity. She taught him about Martin Luther King and the civil rights movement and about Supreme Court Justice Thurgood Marshall and the historic changes in U.S. laws about race. She played Mahalia Jackson's gospel music for him.

She also taught him that his African father was a man of high ideals. Barack, Sr., had grown up poor, but he would never go along with a corrupt system just because it was the practical thing to do. Barry was like his father, she told him, and she was sure he would follow his father's example.

From his mother Barry got the impression that being part black was something to be proud of. However, when he was around nine years old, he came across a magazine article that disturbed him deeply.

It was about an American black man who had tried to lighten his skin with a "miracle" cream. Pictures in the article showed how the chemicals had left his skin patchy and disfigured. It was horrible that the treatment had turned out badly, but it seemed even worse to Barry that the man had wanted so desperately to be white. Barry didn't talk to anyone about this, but it started him thinking.

Lolo was now working for Mobil Oil as a government relations consultant, a well-paying job. In 1970 he was able to buy a house in a better neighborhood, where the streets were paved and the houses were securely walled off from beggars and thieves. Barry had now studied at the Catholic school for three years, but after the family moved he began attending a government-run school.

This school, State Elementary School Menteng 1, offered religious instruction once a week. Barry was registered as Muslim, because his stepfather was considered Muslim, so he attended the Muslim class. He sometimes made faces during the study of the Koran, which meant no more to him than the prayers at his Catholic school had. When his teacher complained to his mother, Ann explained to Barry that he should be respectful of others' beliefs and behave himself during religion class. Ann wasn't at all religious, but she thought it was good for children to be exposed to different faiths.

Outside religion classes, the government school encouraged the children to celebrate the holidays of other religions as well as Islam. They put up decorations for both Christmas and Eid al-Adha, an Islamic holiday. Unlike the custom at traditional Muslim schools, the boys and girls were not separated, and the girls did not wear head scarves. Many of the women teachers wore Western-style clothes such as sleeveless dresses.

Barry's new school was supposed to be one of the best in Jakarta, but Ann was dissatisfied with the education he was getting. She was afraid her early morning English lessons with Barry wouldn't make up for second-rate schooling. Barry seemed to be spending too much of the school day sitting in the back of the classroom drawing superheroes, like Batman and Spider-Man. Ann worried more and more about the limited opportunities he would have if he stayed in Indonesia.

Then there was the time Barry came home with a long, deep gash in his arm. Playing on a mud slide with a friend, he'd ripped his arm open on a barbed-wire fence. Barry wasn't worried about the injury, and neither was his stepfather, but Ann borrowed a car and rushed Barry to the hospital. Even the two doctors at the hospital weren't very concerned. They finished their game of dominoes before sewing Barry's wound up with twenty stitches. The incident caused

Ann to realize that her son might not receive proper medical care in this country.

She was concerned about Barry's values, too. In Jakarta, corruption and going along with the unfair system were facts of life. When she and Barry first arrived at the Jakarta airport, Lolo bribed the customs guards so that they didn't have to wait in the long lines. When the tax officials came to inspect Lolo's house, he hid the refrigerator so that it wouldn't be counted on his tax bill.

Everyone in Indonesia did their best to get around inconvenient rules, but Ann didn't want Barry's character formed by such attitudes. She wanted him to value honesty, fairness, and independent judgment, as her parents had taught her. A hard life wasn't an excuse for low standards. Look at Barack Obama, Sr., who came from a poor, uneducated family but still dedicated his life to working for the benefit of the Kenyan people.

Some of Ann's teachings must have rubbed off on Barry. His third-grade teacher, Fermina Sinaga, later remembered an essay he wrote about what he wanted to be when he grew up. "He wanted to be president," she said. "He didn't say what country he wanted to be president of. But he wanted to make everybody happy."

In the summer of 1970, Barry flew back to Hawaii to spend his vacation with his grandparents. They, too, were concerned about Barry's education, and they took him to interview at Punahou School, a prestigious private school in Honolulu. In the summer of 1971, Ann sent Barry back to Hawaii to begin attending Punahou in the fall. For the time being, he would live with his grandparents.

As for Ann, she promised to join Barry within a year, maybe by Christmas. Ann was disappointed in Lolo. When she fell in love with him in Hawaii, he'd had high ideals about a life of service to the Indonesian people. She had thought they would work together to improve his country. But he had given up his ideals, while she felt more and more deeply for the poor people of Indonesia. Ann and Lolo had drifted apart, and this marriage, too, would soon end.

Chapter 3

Back to Hawaii

Barry's grandparents Madelyn and Stanley had begun their marriage with an elopement, just as his mother and father had done. Madelyn's parents were conventional, respectable citizens of Augusta, Kansas, and Stanley Dunham was an adventurous young man from El Dorado with a salesman's charm and a bad reputation. Madelyn's parents had disapproved of him even more than the Dunhams later disapproved of the African graduate student Barack Obama. So Stanley and Madelyn had gotten married secretly, a few weeks before Madelyn graduated from high school in 1940.

Ann, the Dunhams' only child, had been born in Fort Leavenworth, Kansas, in 1942, during World War II. Stanley Dunham was in the army at the time, and he was shipped off to France to fight under General

Patton. Madelyn worked at the Boeing aircraft plant in Wichita.

After the end of World War II in 1945, the Dunhams moved around the country: California, Texas, Kansas, the state of Washington. Madelyn and Stanley weren't especially aware of the racial discrimination that was common everywhere in the United States at that time. However, they believed in being polite and considerate to everyone, and they were appalled at the harsh racial segregation they found in Texas.

When Madelyn spoke politely to the black janitor at the bank where she worked, a fellow employee scolded her sharply for doing so. At the store where Stanley sold furniture, the other salesmen explained to him that African Americans and Mexicans were not allowed in the store during regular hours. They could buy furniture, but they had to look at it after hours, when there were no white customers in the store.

When the Dunhams finally settled in Hawaii in 1960, they appreciated the multicultural way of life in the islands. In Hawaii, whites had always been in the minority, and many in the population were of mixed race. The Dunhams shopped at a neighborhood market run by a Japanese American; they were invited over for poi and roast pig by native Hawaiian fellow employees of Stanley's; Stanley played checkers in the park with old Filipino men.

In 1971, when Barry returned from Indonesia to attend school in Honolulu, Stanley and Madelyn Dunham were eager to do everything they could for their grandson. Stanley's employer, a Punahou School alumnus, had helped by recommending Barry for admission. The school accepted Barry and gave him a partial scholarship, but his family had to pay the rest of his tuition.

Ann, in the process of separating from Lolo, had no money to spare. Barry's grandparents didn't have much more. They moved from their large house near the University of Hawaii campus to a two-bedroom apartment. Stanley Dunham now worked as a life insurance salesman, a job he disliked and didn't do well at. Fortunately, Madelyn had been promoted to vice president at the Bank of Hawaii, so she could manage to pay the balance of Barry's tuition fees.

Stanley and Madelyn Dunham were proud that Barry was attending Punahou, a high-ranking college-preparatory school founded in 1841. Besides its academic excellence, Punahou boasted a beautiful, secluded campus, with several acres of broad lawns and shady paths. Green hills overlooked the classroom buildings, theaters, tennis courts, and swimming pools.

After four years in Indonesia, Barry felt like an outsider at first. His classmates all knew one another, having attended Punahou since kindergarten. Barry seemed to be wearing the wrong clothes, and his classmates played football—the soccer he'd played in Indonesia wouldn't become a popular sport in the United States for years. The other students came mainly from well-to-do families. While Barry and his grandparents lived in a nondescript concrete high-rise apartment building, most of his classmates lived in spacious houses with backyard swimming pools.

At the age of six, the last time Barry had lived in Honolulu, he'd felt perfectly comfortable as part of Hawaii's ethnic melting pot. His grandfather Stanley used to tease tourists on the beach by telling them with a straight face that Barry was the great-grandson of the Hawaiian king Kamehameha. He thought it was a great joke when they solemnly took a picture of the boy playing in the sand to paste in their photo albums back home.

But now ten-year-old Barry was more aware of racial differences and discrimination. He began to notice that there weren't many African Americans in Hawaii. In Barry's fifth-grade class, there was only one other black child, a girl. A few of the students at Punahou were of Asian heritage, but most of them were white.

During Barry's first semester, his mother did join him in Honolulu as she'd promised. But much more momentous, Barry learned that he was going to meet a man he'd been hearing about for years: his own father. Barack, Sr., was coming to Hawaii for a month at Christmastime 1971 to visit his American son. The Dunhams arranged for him to stay in an apartment in their building.

Barry had last seen Barack Obama, Sr., when he was two years old, too young to remember. He knew he was supposed to be delighted about seeing his father, but instead he felt confused and resentful. He learned that his father had married again for the third time and had six other children—five boys and a girl—in Kenya.

Over the years Ann had worked hard to build up the bond between Barry and his father. Ann had written many letters to Barack about Barry, and she'd always praised her ex-husband to Barry.

Stanley, too, had talked about Barry's father as a supremely confident, commanding man.

Now Ann assured Barry that he and his father would be "great friends," and she tried to prepare him for the visit with information about Kenya. The country had gained independence from British rule in 1963, under the leadership of Jomo Kenyatta, who was still the president in 1971. Kenya was a mixture of many different ethnic groups. While Jomo Kenyatta was from the Kikuyu tribe, Barack, Sr., was from the Luo tribe. The Luo had come to Kenya several hundred years earlier from the Nile River region.

Barry didn't pay close attention, but he got the impression that his father's tribe had originally come from ancient Egypt. That sounded exciting, and at first he was eager to learn more about the Luo. But then Barry read in a library book that the Luo were cattle-herders who lived in mud huts. This was nothing like the pyramids and chariots he'd hoped for. Ashamed, he didn't want to know any more.

When Barack, Sr., finally arrived in Honolulu, Barry still felt confused. His father was tall and very thin. He walked with a cane, because he was recovering from a car accident. As the visit went on, Barry still felt uncomfortable around his father and found it hard to talk to him. They were strangers.

Barry did notice how his mother and grandparents responded to Barack. Something magnetic about him seemed to liven up the air when he was in the room. At first, the four adults enjoyed one another's company, and everyone got along. But after a few weeks, tensions built up.

One evening Barry started to watch a children's Christmas special on TV, *How the Grinch Stole Christmas!* Barack, Sr., ordered him to turn the TV off and study instead. Barry's father assumed he had the authority to give such commands, but his mother and grandmother protested. The adults began to argue bitterly, no longer trying to be polite, while Barry listened from the other room.

Barack accused Barry's grandparents of spoiling him. Stanley was indignant that Barack would try to take charge in *his* house. Madelyn thought her ex-son-in-law had some nerve to come there and give orders, when he'd left Ann and their little son to fend for themselves eight years ago. (She didn't add that she worked full-time at the bank, and she was tired of waiting on Barack.) Ann, who wanted everyone to love and understand one another, reproached Barack for being too tough with Barry, and her parents for never changing.

After this scene, Barry just wanted his father to leave so that he and his mother and grandparents could return to their peaceful life. But then Barry's teacher invited Barack, Sr., to come to Punahou and talk to the fifth graders about Kenya. At first Barry dreaded the visit. Besides the fact that he felt uncomfortable around his father, he was afraid Barack, Sr., wouldn't measure up to the heroic reputation Barry had created for him. Barry had made the mistake of bragging to his classmates that his father was an African prince, and now the truth about the mud huts would come out.

However, on the day that Barack, Sr., spoke to the students at Punahou, Barry was proud. His classmates were impressed with his tall father, looking dignified in his blue blazer. Barack spoke to them in his deep, velvety voice of Kenyan legends and of how Kenya gained its independence from British rule. They listened, mesmerized. By the end of the presentation, Barry was smiling.

At Christmas, Barry gave his father a tie, and his father gave him a basketball. And then before he left, Barack, Sr., gave his son one last present: a recording of

African music. Even better, Barack played the record for Barry and showed him how to dance like a Luo.

When Ann returned to Hawaii to live, she brought Barry's half-sister Maya with her.

She had left Lolo Soetoro, although she would remain on friendly terms with him, as she had with Barry's father. She applied for student grants so that she could go back to school at the University of Hawaii and support her children. Ann planned to become an anthropologist, a social scientist who studies different cultures. She already knew she wanted to work in Indonesia, which contained a fascinating array of cultures. Some three hundred separate languages were spoken throughout the country.

The summer after his father visited Barry, Madelyn Dunham took him, his mother, and Maya on a tour of the United States. Barry, almost eleven, had never seen the mainland before. They traveled from Seattle, Washington, to California, where they went to Disneyland. In Arizona they viewed the Grand Canyon.

Then they rode the Greyhound bus east across the Midwest, where Madelyn had grown up and Ann had been born. They traveled north to Chicago on Lake Michigan, where they spent three days. On the way back to the West Coast for the flight home, they stopped in Yellowstone Park.

Back in Honolulu, Barry lived with his mother and Maya in an apartment near the Punahou School campus. Ann was close and loving with her children, but she expected them to do their part. Since Ann was a single parent, she needed Barry to help out by grocery shopping and looking after his little sister.

Maya adored her brother, but as she got older she liked to tease him. A young teenager now, Barry was proud of his carefully arranged Afro hairstyle. One way to get a rise out of him, Maya discovered, was to mess up his hair.

In spite of all the studying and chores, there was time for Ann, Barry, and Maya to have fun together. On weekends the family might hike and picnic in the wooded hills above Honolulu, where waterfalls cascaded down mossy cliffs and red ginger flowers dotted the undergrowth. Ann had a reverence for the wonders of nature, and she was eager to share her awe with Barry and Maya. She might go so far as to wake them up in the middle of the night to look at an especially beautiful moon.

In 1977 Ann was ready to return to Indonesia for her fieldwork in anthropology. She intended to take

Maya and Barry with her. She was still concerned about her children's education, but she planned to send them to a good school in Jakarta, the International School.

Since Ann loved the people and culture of Indonesia, she looked forward to the move, and Maya didn't object. But Barry wanted to stay in Hawaii. He was now in high school at Punahou, and he didn't want to leave his friends. Stanley and Madelyn encouraged Barry to stay, offering to let him have one of their two small bedrooms. Also, although they didn't exactly say so, they let Barry understand that they wouldn't supervise him as strictly as his mother did.

Ann hated the thought of parting with Barry, but she understood how he felt. He had made a big adjustment to Indonesia at the age of six, and then another big adjustment to Hawaii at the age of ten. Naturally he didn't want to go back to Indonesia and readjust all over again.

So Ann and Maya left, and Barry moved in with his grandparents. He would live there until he graduated from high school two years later.

Chapter 4

High School

During his high school years at Punahou, Barry's classmates thought of him as a warm, friendly, low-key kind of guy with a great smile. Bigger than most of his classmates, Barry played football during his freshman year. But he loved basketball more, and that was his main sport throughout high school. He played second string on the varsity team.

Barry's mother, perhaps remembering how serious she'd been as a teenager, wondered if Barry would ever care about anything except basketball. But Barry was like his mother in at least one way—his sense of fairness. As in elementary school in Indonesia, he was genuinely kind. His classmates noticed that he would refuse to go along with the crowd in teasing another student. Standing apart, Barry would give the tormentors a look of disapproval.

In basketball, Barry was a solid, steady player, although not a star. His sense of fairness came out in sports, too. If the coach was keeping the second-string players on the bench too long, Barry would be the one to speak up for them.

Barry's grades were decent, but not outstanding, and his classmates and teachers knew that he could have been a top student with a little more effort. The good life in Hawaii may have had something to do with Barry's lack of seriousness. Hawaii, more than two thousand miles from the mainland United States, seemed peacefully removed from the rest of the world. The weather was always pleasant, the scenery beautiful.

For Barry and his friends, life was an endless round of bodysurfing at Sandy Beach, going to parties, and playing basketball. Besides the varsity games and practice, they played pickup basketball with the young men who showed up at the gym after school. Barry also spent hours practicing basketball shots by himself on a playground near his grandparents' apartment.

There were a few small signs that Barry was an unusual boy. He read a lot of books, and he listened to jazz artists such as Miles Davis and Charlie Parker as well as the pop music that his classmates liked. Once, he surprised the other students in an English class with a poem he wrote. It was about "an old, forgotten man on an old, forgotten road" who "walks a straight line along the crooked world."

In fact, although Barry didn't talk to his friends about it, he was on an identity quest. As he grew up, he also grew more aware of himself as an American with African ancestry, and he searched for a group to identify with. Who was he?

For one thing, Barry was the son of a black African father. His mother had always emphasized what a remarkable, admirable man her first husband was and encouraged Barry to be like him. Barry did think of his father as a kind of hero.

But he had seen his father only once to remember, when he was ten. His father wrote him letters, and Barry wrote back, but they weren't close the way Barry and his mother were. Barry hadn't even met any of his other African relatives, and he certainly didn't feel African.

However, although Barry was close to his white American mother and white American grandparents, he certainly didn't feel white, either. Was he African American, then? But he had no African American family or community.

Barry searched in books to find out who he was and where he belonged. He read all the well-known writers on the struggles of black people in America: W. E. B. DuBois's essays in *The Souls of Black Folk*, Langston Hughes's poems, the novelists Richard Wright (*Native Son*) and Ralph Waldo Ellison (*Invisible Man*), Martin Luther King's speeches, James Baldwin's essays in *The Fire Next Time*, and Malcolm X's *The Autobiography of Malcolm X*.

The African American writer who appealed to Barry most of all at that time in his life was Malcolm X, with his dignity, his confidence, and his stern call for justice. Barry was also deeply impressed at how Malcolm had been able to turn his life around. Still, it bothered him that Malcolm completely rejected his white background on his mother's side. It was one thing for Malcolm, who had never known his white grandfather, to disavow his white family; it would be quite another for Barry to reject his close and loving mother and grandparents, who had cared for him all his life.

Barry knew that because he lived in Hawaii, he wasn't experiencing the same discrimination that most African Americans faced. Of all the fifty states, Hawaii was the most tolerant of racial differences. Barry's own father had said so, Barry discovered. Barry found a clipping, an article the *Honolulu Star-Bulletin* had published in 1963, when his father graduated from the University of Hawaii. At the time Barack, Sr., had noted that other nations could learn something from the way the different races in Hawaii were willing to cooperate.

Stanley Dunham liked to tell a story from the days when Barack, Sr., was still attending the University of Hawaii. One evening Barry's father and Stanley had gone with a group of friends to a bar in Waikiki. While they were having drinks, a white customer in the bar started to complain loudly about Barack, Sr.'s, presence, using racial slurs.

Barry's father, instead of starting a fight, walked over to the white man with a calm smile. With great dignity and authority he explained to the other man that racial discrimination was wrong, foolish, and against the American principle of respecting the rights of everyone. The white man was so ashamed, Stanley said, that he not only stopped complaining but also pulled a hundred dollars out of his pocket and pressed the money on Barack.

Barack's confidence would have been a lot more reassuring, Barry thought, if his father were here.

Meanwhile, Barry couldn't help noticing some evidence of racism even in Hawaii. His tennis coach, for instance, had made a snide remark about Barry's color.

As far as the coach was concerned, Barry didn't have any mixed feelings. He thought the guy was a jerk, and he quit the tennis team. But he was more confused when it came to friends and family. One night when Barry took two white friends to an all-black party, they felt uncomfortable, and before long they asked him to drive them home. In the car one of the friends tried to tell Barry that he now understood a little bit of what Barry must feel all the time, being surrounded by white people.

Instead of appreciating his friend's sympathy, Barry became angry. How could the white boy possibly understand how he felt? Whites were in charge in this society. If they felt uncomfortable, they could just leave the party; whereas if Barry felt uncomfortable, he could do nothing about it.

Then there was the time Barry's grandmother was harassed at a bus stop by a panhandler. Barry's grandfather told him privately, with shame, that his grandmother had been frightened because the man was black. Barry was shaken to think that his own

Toot was afraid of someone just on the basis of his being African American. Later, however, an older black man named Frank suggested a different view to Barry. In Frank's opinion, Barry's grandmother wasn't really wrong to react that way. Considering the long history of racial bigotry in the United States, African Americans had a reason to harbor deep anger against whites. And such anger sometimes led to violence against whites.

Gramps's attitude bothered Barry, too. Stanley Dunham thought of himself as completely free of racial prejudice. It was true that Stanley was on good terms with all his neighbors and acquaintances, whether they were Filipino, Japanese, Polynesian, or black. He spent hours with black friends, playing poker and bridge or just chatting. But Barry was sure that his grandfather didn't really understand these other men, and that he wasn't as close to them as he assumed.

Brooding about all these things, Barry was confused about what conclusions to draw. He believed that his white friends sincerely liked him, and he knew that his white grandparents loved him dearly. But none of them would ever understand what it was like to be black.

In spite of his inner turmoil, Barry was well liked

at Punahou, and most of his friends were white. They never suspected that Barry had any problems. In the afternoons after school, they would often hang out at his grandparents' apartment. It wasn't too far from the school, and Stanley Dunham welcomed the boys' company. They liked Stanley, too.

One reason Barry liked basketball so much was that some of the best professional basketball players were black. Julius "Dr. J" Erving, the star player for the Philadelphia 76ers at the time, was an athlete of exciting grace and style—a magnetic role model. Barry also loved the way he and the other boys could get completely caught up in playing a game. Then it didn't seem to matter what color anyone's skin was or how much money his family had. On the basketball court, at least, Barry felt like he belonged. He was especially good at long jump shots, and his teammates called him "Barry O'Bomber."

While Barry didn't regret staying in Hawaii, he often felt lonely. His mother wrote him loving letters from Indonesia, and he knew she was thinking about him and making plans for his future. But he longed for a mother and father at home. He didn't share these feelings with his classmates, but he talked more freely with an older boy, Keith Kakugawa, also of mixed race.

Meanwhile, through her letters Ann urged her son to keep his grade point average up and think about college. Although Barry generally made Bs, in his last year or so he let his studies slide. His grandparents worried that he might even do something that would land him in jail, but they didn't confront him about his behavior.

At the beginning of Barry's senior year in high school, his mother returned to Hawaii for a while. She was alarmed by Barry's sinking grades, and by the serious trouble that some of his friends had gotten into. She gave Barry a talking-to: It was time for him to give up his lazy frame of mind and break away from the easy life in Hawaii. In order to do something worthwhile with his life, he should aim to go to a good college on the mainland after graduation.

Barry had been thinking that he'd rather take classes in Honolulu, work part-time, and coast along. He argued back, but in the end, his mother made him feel guilty. Pulling himself together, Barry applied to several colleges on the mainland. He won a full scholarship to Occidental College, a small liberal arts school in Los Angeles, and he decided to go there.

In the spring of 1979, Barry graduated from high school. His mother and Maya flew to Hawaii from

Indonesia for the ceremony. In his personal section of the Punahou yearbook, Barry thanked his grandmother and grandfather. Barry was a normal selfabsorbed teenager in some ways, but he'd come to realize how much he owed Toot and Gramps.

The Dunhams had lived in a modest apartment in order to pay the difference between Barry's scholarship and his tuition fees. They'd shared their home with him, putting up with his adolescent sulkiness and thoughtlessness. They'd worried about him day in and day out, as much as if they were his parents. A photo taken on graduation day shows Stanley and Madelyn hugging Barry and beaming with pride.

Chapter 5

On the Mainland

Los Angeles in 1979 was a loose, sprawling city of almost three million. Unlike Hawaii, it had a sizeable population of African Americans—about one-tenth of the population of the city. Although the U.S. Civil Rights Act of 1968 had outlawed segregation in housing, most blacks lived in a few sections of the city such as Watts, East Los Angeles, and South Central.

These inner-city communities had long been plagued with unemployment, substandard schools, and crime. The residents felt that the city government did not respect them or serve them well, and they especially hated and mistrusted the Los Angeles Police Department. Simmering resentments sometimes broke out in violence, the worst being the Watts Riots of 1965.

However, Occidental College was located in Eagle

Rock, a quiet and well-to-do suburb of Los Angeles. The campus streets were lined with eucalyptus trees; the buildings were Spanish-style with red tile roofs. The other black students at Occidental, a small percentage of the student body, were mostly middle class, like Barry.

These students had various points of view on what it meant to be African American. Some of them imitated the street talk of the black ghetto and spouted militant slogans. Others were determined to ignore racial tensions and live their own lives. "They weren't defined by the color of their skin, they would tell you," Obama wrote later in his autobiography. "They were individuals."

But Barry, still searching for a community where he belonged, couldn't ignore his background. He joined the Black Students' Association at Occidental. He started calling himself by his real name, his African father's name: Barack.

Unlike his mother and father, Barack had never been especially interested in politics. But at Occidental, he began to get involved. There was growing concern at Occidental and at other colleges across the United States about South Africa's policy of apartheid, or legal segregation by race.

At that time, South Africa was ruled by the white minority descended from Dutch and British colonists. The blacks in South Africa were by far the majority of the population, but they lived in poverty. By law they could not vote in national elections or own land outside their "homelands," areas similar to the reservations for Native Americans in the United States. Although South Africa as a nation was prosperous, most of the wealth was owned and controlled by whites.

The United Nations had condemned apartheid for many years, but the United States and western European nations had hung back from breaking economic ties with South Africa over this issue. South Africa was an important trading partner for the United States, exporting diamonds, gold, and farm products, and importing machinery and other technology. Ronald Reagan, elected U.S. president in 1980, opposed any attempt to force South Africa to give up apartheid.

The organized resistance to apartheid in South Africa was the African National Congress (ANC), labeled a terrorist group by the U.S. State Department. The best-known leader of the ANC was Nelson Mandela, who had been in prison since 1964. The speech he gave when he was sentenced, "I Am Prepared to Die," was a source of inspiration for oppressed people all over the world. It also inspired Barack and many other college students.

Barack and his activist friends joined the movement to urge Americans to oppose the injustice in South Africa. One tactic was divestment, or refusing to own stock in South African businesses or in U.S. companies who did business in South Africa. Many colleges, including Occidental, owned investments in South Africa, and students began to demonstrate to get the trustees of the college to sell those tainted investments.

At a divestment rally on the Occidental campus, Barack discovered that he had a talent for public speaking. When he got up to talk about apartheid, an issue that could really change many people's lives, he spoke from the heart. He realized that he could make a crowd pay attention to what he was saying. That incident gave him an inkling that he could find his identity by reaching beyond himself, using his intelligence and talents to help other people.

During his two years at Occidental, Barack began to turn his attention away from his own individual search for identity. He was inspired by the example of Nelson Mandela, the imprisoned leader of the ANC in South Africa. He realized that it might be more satisfying to search for his mission in life. What could he do for other people? This had always been his mother's attitude, which she'd tried to pass on to him. Now it began to sink in.

Gradually, Barack spent less of his time partying and playing basketball. He decided not to try out for the school basketball team, because it would take up too much of his time. He still played basketball, but just pickup games for fun and exercise. He didn't necessarily study any harder, but professors were impressed with his intelligence and ability to express his thoughts. There were plenty of other thinkers, students and faculty, to argue with at Occidental, and Barack discovered that he enjoyed debating and was good at it.

One particular instructor at Occidental, political scientist Roger Boesche, urged Barack to study harder and make use of his talents. His course Modern Political Thought was Barack's favorite during his time at Occidental College. But Barack was angry when Boesche gave him a B on one exam, because he knew his actual score was as high as some students who'd received As.

When Barack questioned his grade, his instructor simply said, "You didn't apply yourself." Like Barack's mother, Boesche wanted him to work up to his potential, not just to do well without really trying. The message was that it wasn't all right to just coast on his talents—he had a responsibility to use them well.

The atmosphere in Los Angeles was more mentally challenging for Barack than it had been in easygoing Hawaii. Madelyn Dunham noticed that her grandson became more purposeful about his life during his two years there. He actually told her that he wanted "to leave the world a better place." Maya, who was following in his footsteps at Punahou School, also noticed a new thoughtfulness and sense of focus about her brother.

Barack was attracted to the field of public policy, the study of governmental decisions that can change the circumstances of people's everyday lives. U.S. policy of trading with South Africa, in spite of that country's policy of legal segregation, was a good example of such decisions. Barack was also pulled in the direction of becoming a writer.

By the spring of 1981, Barack felt he was ready for a bigger challenge than Occidental College. He decided to transfer to Columbia University in New York for his last two years of college. While Occidental was an excellent college, it was small. Columbia was a world-renowned university with a diverse student body. Columbia had produced numerous Nobel Prize winners; it was the home of the prestigious Pulitzer Prize for journalism. In the field of public policy, the faculty at Columbia included such names as Zbigniew Brzezinski, former national security adviser to President Jimmy Carter, and Zalmay Khalilzad, who would serve in several presidents' administrations and eventually become the U.S. ambassador to the United Nations.

One of the strongest attractions of Columbia for Barack was its location: New York, one of the great cities of the world, rather than sprawling, decentralized Los Angeles. Also, the black section of New York, Harlem, was famous as a center for black music, literature, and politics. Malcolm X had once thrilled African American audiences with his oratory in Harlem. Musicians Barack loved, like Billie Holiday, had flourished in Harlem. African American writers he admired, including Langston Hughes and Richard Wright, had lived and worked in Harlem. Harlem, Barack felt, might be the place where he would find his African American community.

Chapter 6

New York City

In August 1981 Barack Obama arrived in New York. His goal of finding his place in an African American community seemed reasonable at first, since the Columbia University campus was in uptown Manhattan, at the edge of Harlem. As a transfer student, Barack would live off campus rather than in a dormitory, so he intended to find an apartment in Harlem. But all the available apartments in Harlem were either in an exclusive district, much too expensive for a scholarship student, or in slums.

The biggest divide in New York, Barack found, wasn't between white and black so much as between rich and poor. On the one hand, there was the New York City of skyscrapers, power, and fabulous wealth. On the other hand, there was the New York City of the underprivileged, the hopelessly poor, and the crime-ridden neighborhoods.

Barack managed to find a low-rent apartment not too far from Columbia, but he failed to find a community. Instead, he fell into a solitary way of life, studying and reading on his own. He spent most of his spare time with challenging books such as the Bible, the novels of Herman Melville and Toni Morrison, and the philosophy of Friedrich Nietzsche. While Barack exercised his mind vigorously, he also went for long runs up and down Manhattan to exercise his body. Throughout high school Barack had been big as well as tall, but during his college years he gradually grew leaner and leaner.

Thinking ahead two years to his graduation from college, Barack planned to travel to Kenya and finally see his father again. The idea had come to him while he was still in Los Angeles. Back in high school, he'd stopped writing to his father, and after a while his father had stopped writing to him. But now Barack felt a need to get in touch with his father.

Before Barack left Occidental, he wrote to Barack, Sr., and told him that he wanted to visit Kenya after he graduated from college. His father wrote back, telling him it was important for him to meet the African side of his family, "and also that you know where you belong." Where he belonged was exactly what Barack wanted to know most. However, it didn't occur to him that his father also needed to see him. Barack imagined Barack, Sr., as a wealthy, important man with a happy family life in Kenya.

The summer after Barack's first year at Columbia, his mother and Maya came to New York to visit. They found him in his shabby apartment surrounded by piles of serious books, and not much else. Barack criticized his sister for reading *People*, a magazine of light articles about the lives of celebrities. Evidently he didn't remember how his father had criticized him, at age ten, for wanting to watch *How the Grinch Stole Christmas!* instead of studying.

Hearing that Barack was planning to visit his father after graduation, his mother talked to him at length about her first husband. She didn't want Barack to feel resentful toward his father, to blame him for leaving their family. She explained that she was the one who had divorced Barack, Sr. When he visited them in Hawaii when Barack was ten, he had asked her to come to Kenya with him, but she had refused.

Listening to his mother, Barack was moved that

she cared so deeply for his father. She obviously wanted the best for him, even after the sad failure of their marriage.

At Columbia Barack majored in political science, with an emphasis on international relations. He was studying hard for the first time. The course work and the professors were more challenging at Columbia than at Occidental, and the other students were more competitive and ambitious. Barack became practiced and confident in debating.

During his senior year Barack took a seminar, a class with only eight students, on foreign policy. The focus of the class was on the uses of foreign aid and how wealth flowed between first-world countries, like the United States, and third-world countries, like Kenya. For his senior thesis, Barack chose the topic of Soviet nuclear disarmament. Ever since the end of World War II, the United States and the Soviet Union (controlled by Russia) had been locked in an arms race. Nuclear war and other harm from nuclear weapons had been a constant threat.

President Jimmy Carter had made some progress in negotiating the Strategic Arms Limitation Treaty with the Soviet Union in 1979. But President Ronald

Reagan urged a massive arms buildup. These two different choices in foreign policy could have serious consequences for not only the United States and Russia but also the entire world.

During Barack's last year at Columbia, several months before graduation, his phone rang one morning as he was fixing breakfast. It was his aunt Jane, his father's sister, calling from Nairobi, Kenya. Barack Obama, Sr., had been killed in a car accident. Aunt Jane asked him to call his uncle Roy, who was living in Boston, and let him know.

Barack was so stunned that he didn't know what he felt. All these years he had heard stories about his father, wondered about him, gazed at pictures of him, and been urged to become a noble person like him. Now Barack would not be able to see him to find out what he was really like.

With Barack's father gone, it didn't seem so urgent to go to Kenya, and he put off the trip. He sent condolences to his father's family, though, and asked them to write. His half sister Auma, who had been born in Kenya shortly before Barack was born in Hawaii, was startled to see how much Barack's handwriting looked like their father's.

Auma was Barack, Sr.'s, second child. Auma's

mother, Kezia, was Barack's village wife. Kezia had been pregnant with Auma when Barack, Sr., left Kenya to study at the University of Hawaii. Now Auma wrote back to Barack, and they began a correspondence.

At Columbia, Barack had decided that he wanted to become a community organizer. He didn't know anyone who had that kind of job. He didn't know exactly what a community organizer would do, except that somehow he would help poor black people take control of their lives.

Barack was inspired by the civil rights movement of the late 1950s and early 1960s. He knew that in spite of progress made by Dr. Martin Luther King and others, there was still a lot to be done. He believed that if people in poor neighborhoods worked together, they could better their lives, and he wanted to be part of the process. It seemed like a way for him to belong to a community, a community of people who were cooperating to bring about justice. He longed for that.

Barack also knew that community organizers weren't well paid, so first he needed to pay off his student loans and save some money. After graduating from Columbia in 1983 with high honors, Barack got a job at the Business International Corporation.

This small company published newsletters on international finance and consulted for U.S. firms doing business outside the country. Barack worked as a research assistant and edited a yearbook, *Financing Foreign Operations*. Barack learned a great deal about the business world and international finance.

Barack's work at Business International Corporation was well paid, so he could afford an apartment in a better neighborhood, on the Upper East Side of Manhattan. Wearing a suit and tie and carrying a briefcase to work, using the services of a secretary pool, Barack felt like a different person—and it wasn't the person he'd planned to be. He was more aware than ever of the sharp divide between rich and poor in New York, and he was afraid that if he went over to the rich side, he'd end up with the wrong values.

However, the other black employees—the secretaries and the security guard for the building—urged him to keep on this track toward more money, more power. They told him his ideals of helping poor people were naïve and foolish. And sometimes he wondered if they weren't right.

One day while Barack was working on the computer at Business International, he received a call from his African half sister, who was studying in Germany.

Barack and Auma had been writing off and on since their father's death. Now she was planning to come to the United States for a visit, and she wanted to see him.

Barack was excited and happy—until she called again with bad news. Their half brother David, the younger son of their father's third wife, had been killed in a motorcycle accident. So the news was doubly bad: a half brother whom Barack had never seen was dead, and he and Auma would not be able to meet, at least not for now. Instead of coming to New York, she had to fly to Kenya for David's funeral.

A few months later Barack resigned from the consulting firm and started looking for a job as a community organizer. Although he sent out dozens of résumés, no one seemed to want to hire him. He took a job for a few months with New York Public Interest Research Group, an organization inspired by political activist Ralph Nader. They sent him to City College of New York (CCNY) to work with minority students, but he didn't feel that he was accomplishing much there.

During this period, in 1984, Barack got his first glimpse of the White House. He and student leaders from CCNY traveled to Washington, D.C., to deliver

a petition to the senators and congressmen represent-
ing New York. The petition protested President Ronald Reagan's proposal to cut student aid, which would
hurt many of the low-income college students in
Harlem.

On this first trip to Washington, Barack had just
time enough to visit the National Mall and gaze down
the length of the Reflecting Pool from the Washington
Monument to the Lincoln Memorial. He also made a
point of taking a look at the White House from Pennsylvania Avenue. He was impressed that ordinary citizens could get so close to the president's residence, in
spite of the fact that President Reagan had been shot
and almost killed by an assassin at the beginning of
his term. Barack thought that the openness expressed
Americans' confidence in their democracy.

Back in New York, Barack continued to search
for a job in his chosen field, but he was out of money.
Just as he was thinking of going back to work in the
business world, he got a call from Jerry Kellman, a
community organizer in Chicago. Kellman himself
was white and Jewish. He was looking for a person of
color to work in Chicago's poor black neighborhoods,
where white people were automatically distrusted.

When Kellman and Barack met for an interview,

Kellman was delighted to find a college-educated black man who wanted the low-paying job. Barack, for his part, was eager to pursue his goal of serving society. He left for Chicago in June 1985.

When Ann heard about Barack's new job, she was happy for her son. Although she was on the other side of the world, she felt connected to him because the purpose of their work was similar. By getting to know the poor women in Indonesian villages, she'd learned that acquiring a loom, a sewing machine, or a cow could transform them into self-sufficient small business owners. Years earlier, when Ann was a young woman and Barry was a young boy in Indonesia, they'd shared the frustration of wanting to help people in need but not knowing how. Now they had each found a practical approach.

Chapter 7

Community Organizer

Barack Obama had seen Chicago only once before, on his trip to the mainland with Toot and his mother, the summer he turned eleven. But he'd heard a lot about the lives of African American people in Chicago. A friend from Occidental College had grown up in a close-knit neighborhood on the South Side. And one of his grandfather's friends in Honolulu was a poet who'd lived in Chicago during the Great Depression and the 1940s. Barack had also read Richard Wright's autobiography, *Black Boy*, about his life in Chicago as a young man.

In the first half of the twentieth century, millions of black people had migrated to the North, hoping for better jobs and for relief from the legal segregation and violence of the South. Chicago was a major destination of these migrants, and in the 1980s it held the largest group of African Americans of any U.S. city. As Barack knew, Chicago also had a reputation as the most segregated city in America.

The mid-1980s were a hopeful but also frustrating time for the black population of Chicago. Two years before Barack arrived in Chicago, Harold Washington had been elected the city's first African American mayor. Mayor Washington wanted to institute a progressive program to reform Chicago politics and improve the lives of the poor black population. However, he was fiercely opposed by a majority of the city council.

To add to the tension, many working-class people, white and black, had lost their jobs in the preceding few years. South Chicago used to be a center of heavy industry, but in the early 1980s, Wisconsin Steel, U.S. Steel, and other large manufacturing plants had closed. There were no other well-paying jobs for blue-collar workers to replace the ones that vanished. Driving around Chicago, Barack saw for himself the huge empty, rusting factories.

Jerry Kellman had Barack start working in Roseland, a neighborhood on the Far South Side of Chicago. This part of the city was almost all black, although not all poor. There were blocks of middle-class homes among the blocks of rundown apartment buildings with extremely poor tenants.

A public housing project named Altgeld Gardens was Barack's first assignment. The very location of Altgeld Gardens was depressing. On one side was the polluted Calumet River; on another, the Lake Calumet landfill, one of the largest dumps in the country. Also close by was the city's sewage treatment plant, and its smell was always heavy in the air.

About two thousand people, almost all of them black, lived in Altgeld Gardens. The two-story brick apartment buildings, originally built for industrial workers, were now forty years old. The Chicago Housing Authority (CHA) was supposed to make repairs to crumbling ceilings or broken toilets and heaters, but it might take them months to do the work. Sometimes they didn't show up at all.

Kellman advised Barack to start by meeting with the residents and talking with them. He should listen carefully to learn what changes might make a real difference in their lives. Then he was to help them organize to achieve the change. The idea was for the people in the community to take action for themselves, changing their conviction that nothing could be done. Positive action would give them confidence in their own power, and confidence would then enable them to make other positive changes.

Barack began working out of a little office in a local church, calling dozens of residents to set up interviews. Listening to story after discouraging story, he began to get the big picture. Twenty years earlier, civil rights laws had ended racial discrimination in housing and employment. Many African Americans had then been able to get better jobs and to move their families from crowded parts of the city to homes in Roseland. But whites promptly moved out of these neighborhoods, and property values fell.

After dozens of interviews, Barack concluded that what the people in the Altgeld community cared about most was jobs. Unemployment ran high, especially among young men. Many of them turned to gangs and crime, making the streets unsafe for ordinary citizens.

The volunteer workers grew fond of Barack. They called him "Baby Face" because he was so young, idealistic, and naïve. They watched him discover what they already knew: No one at city hall cared what happened at Altgeld Gardens.

Barack's first bright idea was to work through the black churches in the area. The black churches in Chicago were powerful social forces, and if only they would work together, they could bring about changes that would help all of their people. But one of the South Side pastors, the Reverend Jeremiah A. Wright, Jr., explained to Barack that his bright idea didn't fit reality. The churches, fiercely independent and suspicious of one another, would be impossible to organize.

Barack soon realized the truth of what Wright said. To each pastor, particularly ones with large followings, organizing with other churches meant sharing some of their power. Furthermore, the black pastors were suspicious of Barack—a young man from New York in the pay of white people—trying to tell the pastors what to do.

After months of hard work characterized by failure and frustration, Barack finally enjoyed a small success. The Chicago city government had an employment department, the Mayor's Office of Employment and Training (MET). But there was no job intake and training center on the Far South Side, where the jobs were most desperately needed. Barack arranged a meeting between the director of MET and the residents of Altgeld and the neighborhood involved in the issue.

By the time the meeting was over, the director had agreed to put an MET center in the area. Barack felt deeply gratified, not just for his own success but also for that of the community residents. They had organized, they had taken action, and they had gotten results.

One thing that impressed Barack about the volunteers working with him in discouraging conditions was how many of them drew on their faith for strength. Barack had not been brought up in a religious tradition. Toot and Gramps were both from Christian backgrounds, but they didn't attend church. His mother was respectful of all religions, but she didn't have a faith in any one of them. Barack's father (whom he'd hardly known, anyway) was an atheist. His stepfather, Lolo, was Muslim but didn't practice his faith seriously.

Until Barack came to Chicago, he'd followed his mother's lead of respecting all religions—from a distance. Ann Dunham seemed to be one of those rare people who was deeply spiritual and ethical, but felt no personal connection to an organized religion. That worked for her, and until now Barack hadn't felt a need for religion, either. But now, struggling to serve in the African American community, he realized that he also needed the strength of a faith community. He began dropping in at various churches on Sunday mornings, and he talked to several pastors about his doubts and hopes.

The religious community where Barack seemed to fit in best was Trinity United Church of Christ, a large church in the Hyde Park neighborhood on the South Side of Chicago. The pastor, Jeremiah Wright, was a preacher of personal magnetism who had built his congregation from only ninety members to several thousand. More important to Barack, Wright and his church were committed to the social justice element of Christian belief. Barack had noticed Trinity in the first place because he saw a sign on its lawn protesting apartheid in South Africa.

Also, Wright was an educated, intelligent man, willing to have long discussions with Barack about faith and how it related to the problems of poverty, racism, and injustice. Sitting in the congregation on Sundays, Barack wasn't sure what he believed, but he wanted to be part of this church.

One particular sermon of Wright's, titled "The Audacity of Hope," struck him especially. The pastor spoke forcefully about all the injustice and violence and suffering in the world in general, and the sorrows of this congregation in particular. But then he talked even more forcefully about the hope that keeps people going and allows them to praise God in spite of everything. Everyone in the church was moved, and Barack had tears in his eyes.

During Barack's years as a community organizer in Chicago, his Kenyan half sister, Auma, came to meet him at last. She was living in Germany now, where she'd gone to study after she graduated from high school. To the delight and relief of both of them, they felt close and comfortable with each other from their first hug at the Chicago airport.

Barack showed his sister his little office in the church in Roseland and introduced her to the volunteers who worked with him. Auma told Barack many things about their father, whom she called "the Old Man."

Barack knew part of the story: Barack Obama, Sr., had returned to Kenya in 1965 with a master's degree in economics from Harvard. He got a good job with an American petroleum company, and then he gained appointments in the Kenyan government. Barack had the impression from his father's letters that the Old Man had been a respected and important man in Kenya all his life.

But Auma explained that Kenya, independent from Great Britain for only a few decades, was split over tribal loyalties. The largest tribe in Kenya was the Kikuyus, and the Old Man felt that Jomo Kenyatta favored Kikuyus over the Luo, the Obama family's tribe. The Old Man saw other men promoted over him just because they were Kikuyu. When the Old Man complained, he lost his position in the Kenyan Ministry of Finance.

Meanwhile, the Old Man had brought Auma, four years old, and her older brother, Roy, six, to live with him and his new American wife, Ruth Nidesand, in Nairobi. Ruth and the Old Man eventually had two boys, Mark and David. At first the family was very well-off, with a big house to live in and a Mercedes to drive.

But after the Old Man fell out of favor with the government, he couldn't get another job. No one, not even American companies, would hire an enemy of Kenyatta's. The Old Man drank heavily, and he grew bitter and quarrelsome. Ruth left him, taking Mark and David.

The Old Man became so poor that he and his two oldest children hardly had enough to eat. Roy left home to live with relatives until he finished his education at the University of Nairobi. Auma loyally stuck with her father until she was old enough to escape to Germany to finish her own education. The Old Man suffered a series of car accidents, and finally he died in one.

Listening to Auma's stories, Barack was dazed. In his letters, his father had said nothing about all this. All those years when they were writing back and forth, Barack had imagined his father riding around Kenya in a Mercedes, conferring with top officials. Barack Obama, Sr., in Barack's imagination, had been an exalted role model for his American son. Now Barack realized that his father, although a brilliant man with high ideals, had also been a human being with flaws.

At the end of Auma's stay in Chicago, she and Barack agreed to meet in Kenya some day soon and visit their African family together. Then Auma left, and Barack flew to Washington, D.C., where their older brother, Roy, now lived. Roy added his view to Auma's description of their father: a man with three different families, unable to be a responsible father to any of his children.

Talking with Auma and Roy and watching the African American families on the South Side of Chicago, Barack thought about how different his own life might have been. If he'd lived in Kenya, he might have been like Roy, growing up with a father who was unemployed, angry, and often drunk. Or if Barack had lived in Altgeld Gardens, he might have been like one of the young men he saw hanging around street corners, acting cool and tough, dying at an early age or ending up in prison.

Instead, Barack had always had a secure home with his mother and his grandparents. He had enjoyed an excellent education and a range of job opportunities. He was lucky. More than ever, he was determined to do something for others, to share his good luck.

As a community organizer, one of Barack's biggest successes was a campaign to get the asbestos removed from the apartments in Altgeld Gardens. The Chicago Housing Authority didn't want residents even to know about the asbestos and its dangers, and the residents found out about it only accidentally. With Barack's help, a group of residents confronted the housing authority and demanded the asbestos be removed.

However, as time went on, Barack began to think that community organizing was not the best way for him to make a difference in people's lives. While he could work for months without making any headway at all, the mayor of Chicago could create big changes in schools, neighborhoods, or families just by giving an order. Also, Harold Washington had an important effect on people's lives just because he was a public leader they felt connected to.

Barack could see that this politician was the focus for the hopes and dreams of thousands of people. He noticed Washington's picture on the wall in African American homes and places of business all over southern Chicago. When Mayor Washington died suddenly of a heart attack in November 1987, the black community was grief stricken. They were deprived of a leader who had brought them together and given them pride.

Maybe, Barack thought, the way to make big changes was to get into politics. And the way to get into politics was to earn a law degree. The U.S. government was a system of self-government by laws, and so was the government of Illinois and of the city of Chicago. Politicians like congressmen and senators made laws. Politicians like presidents, governors, and mayors applied the laws. If you knew the laws, you could make them work for the people you represented.

That's how Harold Washington had started, by studying law. So had Abraham Lincoln, for that matter.

Chapter 8

Kenya

In May 1988 Barack quit his community organizer job in Chicago. He'd been accepted at Harvard Law School for that fall, and now he was going to spend the summer traveling. First he toured Europe for three weeks, and then he flew from London to Kenya. He would stay in Kenya for five weeks, getting to know the African side of his family. He hoped that Kenya would help him to better understand his father.

Auma was now teaching at the University of Nairobi, and she picked Barack up at Jomo Kenyatta International Airport. In Nairobi, Barack met his father's sisters, including Aunt Jane, who had called him six years earlier with the news of his father's death. He met Kezia, Obama Sr.'s first wife and Auma and Roy's mother; his half brother Bernard, Kezia's youngest son; and many other aunts, uncles, and cousins. Bernard's older brother Abo was living on the family farm in Kogelo, so Barack would not meet him until later.

The African Obamas welcomed Barack as long-lost family, whether they were actually related to him by blood or not. They all called him "Barry"; that was the name that Barack Obama, Sr., had always used when he talked about his American son. Barack realized that his father had talked about him often, with pride.

Barack's half brother Roy joined the gathering, flying into Nairobi from Washington, D.C. The family celebrated with a feast, including typical Kenyan foods like *chapos* (flat bread), *sukuma wiki* (collard greens), and *ugali* (cornmeal cake).

It was a new feeling for Barack, to be embraced by a huge extended family. It was also a new feeling for him to be in a city—a country, nearly a whole *continent*—full of people who looked like him. In the U.S., the first thing most people noticed about him was that his skin was darker than theirs. Here, people wanted to know first which tribe he belonged to.

Although Barack's father had been dead for several years, Barack almost felt that he was present with him in Nairobi. As he walked the same streets where his father had walked, and talked to the people who had known him, he understood Kenya better, and he understood better what his father's life here had been like.

Barack had seen poverty in Indonesia, New York, and Chicago. But he'd never seen such a concentration of poverty as in Nairobi. One large section on the outskirts of the city was a vast shantytown called Kibera, Africa's worst slum.

Kibera spread across a valley, acre after acre of cardboard and plywood shacks along dirt paths, with open sewers and no clean water. Since the people had no legal right to be there, Nairobi didn't provide any services. Some 500,000 people lived there, and often ten people lived in a one-room hut.

Barack made a special trip to Kibera to meet his aunt Sarah, Barack, Sr.'s, older sister. Sarah and Barack, Sr.'s, mother, Akumu, was their father Onyango's first wife. But Akumu had been unhappy in the Obama family and left them early on. Barack, Sr., had actually been raised by his father's second wife, also named Sarah but called "Granny" by everyone. Recently, Aunt Sarah had quarreled with the rest of the family over the Old Man's inheritance.

There were other family quarrels. Ruth, Barack, Sr.'s, second American wife, had divorced him and separated herself and her two sons from the rest of the family. It was her younger son, David, who had died in a motorcycle accident a few years earlier. She still lived in Nairobi, and she and her older son, Mark, a student at Stanford University in California, now wanted to meet Barack.

Ruth and Mark showed Barack family pictures from the years that Auma and Roy had lived with Ruth, the Old Man, and their children, Mark and David. Barack thought about how different his life might have been if his mother, Ann, had taken him to live with his father in Kenya. Again he considered how lucky he was.

Barack also puzzled over the tangled relationships in the families his father had come from and the families his father had created. The wonderful thing about an African family was that family members were so loyal to one another. Families expected to care for all their members, even a half brother like Barack who had grown up in America.

But family ties could also be burdensome. Auma felt that their father had been dragged down by all the people he felt responsible for—not only his wives and children but all his relatives, all his tribespeople, all of the many people who expected something of him.

Barack could understand that, because he found himself worrying about his young half brother Bernard. At seventeen, Bernard was easygoing and agreeable, but he was even more aimless than Barack had been at the same age. When Barack tried to talk to him about plans for the future, he felt that Bernard seemed to have no ambition at all.

During Barack's second week in Kenya, he and Auma left Nairobi to go on a safari in the Great Rift Valley. It was only a day's trip by van from the capital city to the valley. Barack was thrilled at the sight of the wide plains roamed by lions, giraffes, and hippos, and by great herds of zebras and wildebeests. He was awestruck to think that, according to paleontologists, human beings originated on this very part of the planet.

The heart of Barack's Kenya stay, though, was his visit to the farm, near the village of Kolego in Luo country, where his father had grown up. When Auma visited Barack in Chicago, she had described the family homestead in loving detail: the tree-shaded compound with the cow and the chickens, the smell of smoke from the wood fire, Granny telling amusing stories.

Auma and Roy had spent much of their childhood in Nairobi, but Auma's happiest memories were of the compound in Kolego. "Home Squared," Auma and Roy called it. Your Home Squared was the place your ancestors came from, your true home.

Barack, Auma, and Roy, as well as several other family members, traveled to the farm. First they took a train overnight to the city of Kisumu, near the western shore of Lake Victoria. Then they rode a bus for several hours. The bus was so crowded that Barack had to sit with chickens on his lap.

Getting off at the gold-mining town of Ndori, Barack and the others took a jitney van into the hills. Here, at the farm where the Old Man had been raised, two more uncles met the travelers. Later Barack would also meet his half brother Abo. The uncles led the visitors through the tall hedges that enclosed the family compound, Home Squared.

Besides several small round huts, the compound contained the square main house with concrete walls and a corrugated iron roof, draped with flowering vines. Granny, the woman who had raised Barack Obama, Sr., as her own son, came out to greet them. With a hug, she welcomed Barack as her grandson.

Granny couldn't speak English and Barack couldn't speak the Luo language, but they smiled at each other. They sat down under a mango tree in the center of the compound, and she told him the story of his family. Auma translated, sitting with Barack and their grandmother, as Granny braided her hair. Granny's story started several generations prior, describing the lives and customs of the Obamas before Europeans arrived in Kisumu.

In the course of the story Granny told Barack a great deal about his grandfather, her husband, Hussein Onyango Obama. Barack had imagined him as an independent, proud Kenyan nationalist. After all, he was the man who had written Ann Dunham's parents that he didn't want his son marrying a white woman.

But actually Onyango had worked for many years as a servant to various white men. Granny still had Onyango's official papers from that time, when the British ruled Kenya, a passbook identifying him as a domestic servant. However, Onyango had not remained a servant. Learning modern farming techniques, he had developed the land that the family now lived on. He had turned a tract of unproductive bush into a self-sustaining farm.

Barack's grandfather and father were both buried behind the house, near a cornfield. Their graves were two cement slabs side by side. Barack sat between the graves and shed tears, and he finally felt that he'd found the connection he'd been looking for all his life.

During their stay in Kolego, Auma took a picture of Barack sitting beside Granny. In the photo, both of them are smiling happily. He is leaning toward her, while she strokes his hair with one hand.

Chapter 9

Law School and Michelle

Entering Harvard Law School in September 1988, Barack Obama was twenty-seven. He was older than most of his classmates, and his experience was broader. Although he hadn't accomplished nearly as much as he'd wanted to as a community organizer, he had learned a great deal from his years in Chicago. His trip to Kenya, too, had helped him sort out how he intended to use his life. He now had a clearer idea of his goals, and he had the discipline to achieve them.

Barack spent most of his three years of law school in the library, reading, studying, and writing. Researching legal cases and statutes was often tedious, and sometimes the legal arguments were over petty details. Barack saw, also, that laws could be used by people with power merely as a way to control the people without power. However, the main result of his studies was to deepen his respect for the law, especially the constitution, the undergirding of the U.S. legal system. Later, he described American law as the record of "a long-running conversation, a nation arguing with its conscience."

While Barack studied the law, he also worked as a research aide for a professor, the famous legal scholar Laurence Tribe. This was valuable experience, because Tribe was one of the foremost liberal constitutional law experts in the country. He frequently presented cases before the U.S. Supreme Court. Tribe later remembered Barack Obama as his "most amazing research assistant."

At the end of his first year of law school, Barack was selected as one of the seventy student editors of the *Harvard Law Review*. This was an honor, because the editors were selected on the basis of their first-year grades and their entry in a writing competition, as well as recommendations from instructors and other students.

The early 1990s was a period of racial discord at Harvard. A group of black students confronted the university, asking for more minority representation on the faculty. Derrick Bell, an African American and a tenured professor at Harvard Law School, resigned his position in 1992 in protest over the lack of women of color among the faculty. Barack was deeply impressed with Bell's action, and he gave a speech praising Bell and calling for a more representative faculty; otherwise, he was not much involved in the disputes over racial issues.

Barack was active in the Black Law Students Association, but he made good friends among both black and white students. His focus for the most part was on combating injustice for poor people. At one meeting of the black students at Harvard's law, medical, and business schools, the topic of discussion was whether they wanted to call themselves "black" or "African American." Barack's opinion was that it didn't matter very much. As his friend Cassandra Butts remembered it, he told the meeting, "You know, whether we're called black or African Americans doesn't make a whole heck of a lot of difference to the lives of people who are working hard, you know, living day to day, in Chicago, in New York."

Barack took part in the antiapartheid movement on the Harvard campus. In the years since his Occidental College days, when he first realized what an important issue apartheid was, there had been some hopeful developments for South Africa. In 1986, Congress had passed the Comprehensive Anti-Apartheid Act over President Reagan's veto. This law banned all new U.S. trade and investment in South Africa. The law was to remain in effect until the white South African government eliminated apartheid and released ANC leader Nelson Mandela from prison.

At the end of his second year, in 1990, Barack was elected president of the *Harvard Law Review*. This was a great honor, and the competition was fierce. As the first African American president of the *Harvard Law Review*, Barack made the national news after his election was announced in February.

Barack was chosen as president partly because of his high-quality work in his courses but also because he had a reputation for not taking sides in the bitter political and personal arguments that raged through the law school. Although Barack was politically liberal, conservatives respected him as a fair-minded thinker. He could see their point of view, even if he didn't agree with it. Since he had to manage the seventy strong-willed student editors, as well as all the other legal writers who wanted to be published in the *Harvard Law Review*, this fair-minded approach served him well. His policy as president was to allow a range of opinions to be expressed, to encourage the editors to work together, and to maintain the high quality of the journal.

While Barack Obama was progressing toward a law degree, his personal life changed dramatically. During the summer of 1989, after his first year of law school, he worked as a summer associate at the Chicago law firm of Sidley Austin. The attorney who was assigned to show him around the firm and help train him was the only African American attorney in the office: Michelle Robinson.

Barack was smitten at first sight. Michelle, a tall, confident young woman with striking looks, was more skeptical of him—she could see that he was intelligent, ambitious, and charming, but she was looking for deeper qualities. Besides, she didn't think it was appropriate to date someone she worked with.

But Barack persisted, and Michelle warmed up to him. Their first date was to see Spike Lee's movie *Do the Right Thing*, about racial conflict in a multiethnic neighborhood in Brooklyn, New York. The more Michelle got to know Barack, the more impressed she was by his unusual background, his work as a community organizer, and his plans for the future. She realized that he was a deep-thinking person with high ideals.

As for Barack, he was almost as attracted to Michelle's family as he was to her. She'd grown up in a close-knit black community in Chicago. Her parents, Frasier and Marian Robinson, were also both from Chicago. The Robinsons had raised Michelle and her older brother, Craig, in a four-room bungalow on the South Side. Frasier worked as a city pump operator, in spite of being handicapped by multiple sclerosis, while Marian stayed home to raise the children.

Michelle's mother and father hadn't gone to college, and they were determined that their children would have the chance for a better education. They encouraged Michelle and Craig to work hard and respect their teachers, but also to think for themselves. Craig went to Princeton University on a basketball scholarship, and two years later Michelle also entered Princeton. After graduation from college, Michelle went on to Harvard Law School, graduating two years before Barack.

Barack admired the Robinsons, and he loved their stable, happy family life. While Barack was close with individual members of his family—for instance, he spent hours on the phone with his younger half sister,

Maya—the family as a whole was fragmented and scattered over the globe.

The fact that Michelle's brother, Craig, was a former college basketball star was just icing on the cake to Barack. The two young men played pickup games together for fun, and Craig was impressed with Barack's confidence on the court. Craig was a much better player who could have made a career of professional basketball, but Barack was still eager to test his skills against Craig's.

During Barack's last two years at Harvard Law School, he and Michelle grew closer and closer. When Michelle's father died, Barack flew to Chicago to be with Michelle at the funeral.

In the spring of 1991, Barack graduated with high honors from Harvard Law School. He moved back to Chicago and passed the Illinois bar exam, required in order to practice law. There hadn't been much doubt that he would pass the exam, but he took Michelle out to dinner to celebrate. That night, he proposed marriage, and she accepted.

After they were engaged, Barack took Michelle to Hawaii and introduced her to his grandparents. Stanley Dunham was very taken with Michelle's good looks. Madelyn, always no-nonsense herself, cared more about whether her grandson's fiancée had a level head on her shoulders. She praised Michelle as "a very sensible girl."

Barack also took Michelle to Kenya so that she could meet the African side of his family. When they visited Granny in Kolego, the older Kenyan woman and the young American woman took to each other immediately. All the Obama relatives liked Michelle, in fact, and they were pleased that she quickly picked up a number of words and phrases in the Luo language.

Michelle had always wanted to visit Africa, the place her ancestors came from. However, from this trip she learned how American she was, and how glad she was to be American. Kenyans could be put in jail just for publishing criticisms of the government. Kenyans who wanted to start a business, or even get a job, had to bribe someone in power first.

For Barack, too, visiting Kenya again under-scored his appreciation of his own country. From his years of studying law, he had a deeper understanding of the U.S. constitution and system of government. Barack saw, more than ever, that American democ-racy depended on equal opportunity and justice, and he was determined to work for these values.

Barack Obama and Michelle Robinson were

married in October 1992. It was sad that Michelle's father hadn't lived to see this day. Barack's grandfather Stanley Dunham, too, died before the wedding.

Otherwise, the wedding was a joyous occasion. Jeremiah Wright, their pastor and by now a good friend, performed the ceremony at Trinity Church. Their family and friends gathered from around the country and from all over the world. Just on Barack's side of the guest list, Toot was there from Hawaii, Ann from Indonesia, Maya from New York, where she had just moved, Auma from Nairobi, and Roy from Washington, D.C., plus friends from Honolulu, Occidental College, New York, Chicago, and Harvard.

After the wedding, Barack and Michelle moved into a condominium in Hyde Park, a middle- to upper-class, racially mixed section of Chicago. Barack intended to join a law firm, but first he finished directing Illinois Project Vote, a program to register new voters in Chicago. It was an important election year, with President George H. W. Bush, Republican, running for reelection against Democrat Bill Clinton, governor of Arkansas.

Project Vote succeeded in registering almost 150,000 new voters, most of them black. That November, they helped elect Bill Clinton to the presidency. They also elected Carol Moseley Braun, a lawyer and

Illinois state representative, the first African American woman to become a U.S. senator.

In 1993, Barack joined the law firm of Davis, Miner, Barnhill & Gallard in Chicago. They specialized in civil rights and discrimination cases. Barack, with his outstanding record at Harvard, was sought after by many law firms, and he could have made much more money practicing corporate law. But civil rights and discrimination cases were exactly the kind of work he wanted to do.

At the same time, Barack began working on a book. A publisher had already given him a contract and an advance for a book in 1991, when he made news as the first black president of the *Harvard Law Review*. In the fall of 1992, the University of Chicago, hoping to lure Obama as a permanent faculty member, offered him a fellowship and an office where he could work on the book.

Barack didn't set out to write a memoir, an account of his personal experiences. He intended his book to be an important analysis of race relations in the United States. He thought he'd finish it in one year. But the more he wrote, the more the book became his own personal story, and the more difficult it was to keep on schedule.

Through the writing, Barack explored his often confused and contradictory feelings about his background. He was the child of a white American mother and a black Kenyan father. He'd grown up in Hawaii and (for a few years) Indonesia, far from the mainland United States and Kenya. He'd experienced racial discrimination, but nothing like the oppressive segregation and prejudice that most black people in the United States were familiar with.

It was a lot to sort out, and it took Barack more than twice as long as he expected, even though he often stayed up late at night to work on the book. He wrote in a cramped room off the kitchen that Michelle called "The Hole." Michelle thought he was trying to accomplish too much at once, between a full-time job and an ambitious writing project.

Michelle Obama was a high achiever herself, at the time the founding director of the Chicago office of Public Allies. This public service program recruited, trained, and placed young people from diverse backgrounds in paid internships with nonprofit organizations. However, whatever her commitments, Michelle firmly believed in reserving time for a personal life with family and friends.

Chapter 10

Into Politics

While Barack Obama was writing his book, he often consulted his mother to get the facts of his early life straight. Ann Dunham Sutoro (she had kept her second husband's last name, but changed the spelling) had lived in Indonesia for many years now. She had received a PhD from the University of Hawaii in anthropology. She worked energetically to better the condition of women in developing countries.

Ann had been one of the first to promote microcredit, or very small loans, to poor but enterprising women to help them start small businesses. With only enough money to buy a loom or a sewing machine, a woman could earn enough to lift herself and her family out of poverty and send her children to school. For such a small investment, microloans had an impressive effect for good. The idea caught on, and many governments as well as nonprofit organizations put it to use.

In 1994 Barack finished his book, which by now had turned into a full-fledged memoir titled *Dreams from My Father: A Story of Race and Inheritance*. The title fit the book well. Its major theme was Barack trying to connect with his missing father and his African background.

About the same time that *Dreams from My Father* came out, Ann discovered that she was seriously ill with cancer. She moved back to Hawaii, where her mother cared for her. Ann died at the age of fifty-two in November 1995, only a few months after Barack's book was published. Barack flew to Hawaii to be with his half sister Maya and his grandmother Madelyn. They scattered Ann Dunham Sutoro's ashes from cliffs overlooking the surf on the South Shore of Oahu.

Barack was sorry that he hadn't realized how close Ann was to death, and that he hadn't been with her when she died. He also regretted that he hadn't included more in *Dreams from My Father* about his mother, a remarkable woman who gave him his deepest values. "I know that she was the kindest, most generous spirit I have ever known," he wrote later in a preface to the 2004 edition of *Dreams*, "and that what is best in me I owe to her."

The first edition of *Dreams from My Father* received good reviews. *The New York Times Book Review* praised the way the book described "the phenomenon of belonging to two different worlds, and thus belonging to neither." *The Washington Post Book World* said, "Fluidly, calmly, insightfully, Obama guides us straight to the intersection of the most serious questions of identity, class, and race." However, *Dreams from My Father* sold less than 10,000 copies—not exactly a bestseller. The paperback edition sold even less, and the book went out of print.

But by now Barack was finished with writing about his past and was well into launching his political career. In 1995, when he was thirty-three, his first chance came up to run for an elected office. Alice Palmer, the state senator for the Thirteenth District, decided to run for Congress. That left her seat in the state legislature open.

Michelle was skeptical about a political career for her husband. She disliked politics and she doubted that Barack would succeed—she thought he was too idealistic. But she supported him because he wanted so much to try and because she respected his goal of working for important reforms.

Barack started to put together a campaign. He would need an enthusiastic team of volunteers to work for his election, a network of influential people who would back his candidacy, and donors to fund the campaign. Judson Miner, a senior partner in the law firm where Barack worked, had been Mayor Washington's legal counsel, and Miner had many valuable contacts to share. Barack also had his own contacts from his successful direction of Project Vote in 1992. And Michelle, who had lived in Chicago all her life and had worked for Mayor Richard M. Daley as an aide, connected Barack with some influential people in the city.

A backer who raised about a tenth of the funds for Obama's campaign was Tony Rezko, a real estate developer. Obama was in favor of Chicago's policy to give developers tax credits for developing low-income sections of the city. With the tax credits, renovating run-down neighborhoods became an attractive business opportunity for developers like Rezko. And the city benefited from upgrading those sections.

When Obama announced his candidacy in September 1995, Alice Palmer herself endorsed him as her replacement. But a few months later, when it seemed that she would lose the Democratic primary for the U.S. House of Representatives, she decided to go for her old seat instead. She asked Barack Obama to bow out of the race at this point, but he refused. Now Palmer turned from his most important backer into his main opponent.

Alice Palmer would probably have won her state senate seat back, except that Obama's campaign challenged her nominating petitions. In order to get on the ballot, a candidate must have a certain number of registered voters sign his or her petitions. The signatures, to be valid, must be written in cursive script, not printed.

Because Palmer had made the decision to run for state senate at the last minute, her signatures had been gathered hastily. Not enough of them were valid, and so she was disqualified from running. In fact, all of the other Democratic candidates were disqualified, too, by irregularities in their petitions. Obama ran unopposed in the Democratic primary. Since the Thirteenth District was heavily Democratic, he won the general election in November by a wide margin.

However, Obama was not welcomed with open arms when he took office in Springfield, the capital of Illinois. Some black politicians close to Alice Palmer felt he should have stepped aside rather than running against her. They thought Obama was more interested in his own ambition than in the good of the black community. At one point, another state senator heckled Obama so badly that they had a shouting match on the floor of the senate.

Another reason for Illinois legislators to dislike Obama was that he was critical of Illinois state politics. They resented his attitude. The fact that Obama had a law degree from Harvard only made them think of him as elitist.

There was a great deal to criticize about Illinois politics, which had a reputation for corruption. Also, there was continual fighting between groups: between Democrats and Republicans, and among the representatives of different districts. Obama wondered, with all the problems facing the state as a whole, why couldn't the politicians work together to solve them? For instance, unemployment was a problem for whites as well as blacks.

Some in the black community mistrusted Obama's approach. For many years, black politicians had had to struggle against the white power structure to achieve anything for their people. Now Obama was saying that multicultural cooperation was the best way for both blacks and whites to make progress.

That sounded like he was going over to the other side. The fact that many of his backers were white liberals made some blacks even more suspicious.

However, Obama went quietly to work. In 1998, he helped to get a campaign finance reform law passed in the Illinois legislature. The law, which prohibited legislators from accepting gifts from state contractors or lobbyists, passed the state senate easily. But Obama made some enemies among politicians who had benefited from such gifts.

Gradually, Obama got a reputation in the Illinois senate, at least among Republicans and downstate Democrats, for fair and reasonable dealing. "The most important thing that you do in Springfield is you bring all sides of an issue to the table and you make them feel they are being listened to," he explained to a journalist. It was the same approach that had worked well for Obama back at Harvard Law School, when he was the president of the *Harvard Law Review*.

Obama also made an effort to socialize with his fellow legislators. He began to play golf, a popular sport among the politicians. He joined a running poker game, which helped him make some friends among Republicans as well as Democrats, even though he often won. He still played basketball for fun and exercise, sometimes with a fellow legislator.

In 1998, Barack and Michelle Obama's daughter Malia Ann was born on the Fourth of July. In the midst of his joy, Obama was determined to be the kind of father that he wished he'd had. Writing *Dreams from My Father*, he'd thought long and hard about his childhood.

Barack's father had left him and his mother. His stepfather had withdrawn as Barack grew older. His grandfather hadn't been able to make a good living, and his grandmother had supported the three of them. Barack didn't doubt that his father, his stepfather, and his grandfather Dunham had all loved him, but he felt he could do better by his own children.

As Obama quickly realized, being a good father and husband was not easy to balance with being a dedicated politician. For one thing, the legislature was in Springfield, two hundred miles from their home in Chicago. Barack often had to be away from home overnight, leaving Michelle to change diapers and get up when the baby cried in the middle of the night.

Michelle cut back her work to a part-time job at the University of Chicago, but even so, she was tired and stressed. Barack, besides his work as state senator, still taught constitutional law at the University of Chicago. When he was home, he had paperwork to do or evening meetings to go to.

In spite of concerns about his family life, Obama didn't give up his ambition to rise in the political world. During his first two-year term, he took some time to travel around the southern half of Illinois. The people there weren't his constituents, but some of the issues he voted on in the legislature affected them, too. Also, they might become his constituents in the future, if he ran for a statewide office.

In contrast to the big city of Chicago, central and southern Illinois were made up of farming communities and small cities. Although those areas were mainly Republican, middle-class, and white, Obama found that he felt comfortable with the downstate voters. In fact, they reminded him of his grandparents from the Midwest, Stanley and Madelyn Dunham.

Chapter 11

State Senator Obama

Barack Obama never intended to remain in the Illinois state senate forever. Originally, he'd thought he would follow in Harold Washington's footsteps to become a progressive mayor of Chicago. But by now Richard M. Daley was mayor, and he seemed to have a firm political hold on the city for the foreseeable future. It would be foolish, Barack judged, to try to challenge Daley.

However, Obama thought he saw a good opportunity to run for U.S. House of Representatives in 2000. Obama had the impression that the current congressman for the First District, Representative Bobby Rush, could be unseated. Obama didn't think Rush had accomplished much during his several years in Congress. Obama felt he couldn't pass up such a good political chance, even though he and Michelle were in the middle of adjusting to parenthood.

But before long Obama realized that Congressman Rush was more secure in his seat than he'd first assumed. For one thing, all the voters knew who Bobby Rush was, while hardly any of them had heard of Barack Obama. Not only that but the polls showed voters giving Rush a good solid 70 percent approval rating.

Rush was unquestionably part of the black community he represented. He'd worked in the civil rights movement of the 1960s. He was a former member of the Black Panthers, an organization formed to promote civil rights and self-defense for African Americans. Also, Rush had been a close political ally of the late beloved black mayor of Chicago, Harold Washington.

Obama, in contrast, was easily portrayed by his opponents as "not black enough." It wasn't so much about his white mother as it was about his elite Columbia and Harvard education and the fact that he talked as if he were white. Furthermore, some of his biggest campaign contributors were well-to-do whites, like the real estate developers who were reaping profits from turning run-down South Side neighborhoods into upscale areas. Such development was resisted by black activists, since one effect was poor black renters being pushed out of these neighborhoods.

Another drawback for Obama was his lack of campaign funds. Running for U.S. representative took much more money than running for state senator. Especially since he wasn't well-known, Obama needed a good media blitz to get his name into voters' heads. In order to run enough television ads, he'd need at least $200,000 a week. But his fund for the entire campaign amounted to only $600,000.

Besides these disadvantages, Obama had two strokes of bad luck. First, Bobby Rush's son was shot and killed on the street. There was a flood of public sympathy for Rush, the grieving father. In other circumstances, the best tactic for an underdog like Obama to beat a frontrunner like Rush would have been to attack him vigorously. But now it would look very bad if Obama criticized his rival, so he held back.

Next, in December 1999, Obama, Michelle, and Malia (then almost a year and a half old) left for a vacation in Hawaii. Christmas in Hawaii with his grandmother, now in bad health, was a longstanding tradition for Barack. This year, he and Michelle needed the vacation more than usual, with the added strains of his campaign and of caring for a toddler. Barack originally planned to stay in Hawaii for two weeks, but he cut the trip to five days because of his campaign schedule.

Unfortunately, while Obama was away, an important vote came up in the Illinois senate: the Safe Neighborhoods gun-control bill. The murder rate in Chicago was higher than ever, and the issue was underlined by Bobby Rush's son's recent death by shooting. Voters in Obama's district supported the measure, and so did he—he'd always been in favor of gun control.

Obama's campaign manager, Dan Shomon, urged him to fly back to Illinois for the vote. That was what Obama wanted to do, since he knew the vote would be close. But Michelle was unhappy that he was spending so much time away from the family, and now Malia had come down with a bad cold. Obama stayed in Hawaii—and the Safe Neighborhoods measure failed to pass by three votes.

Returning the following week at the beginning of January 2000, Obama explained to the media about his commitment to his grandmother, his wife, and his sick child. But only one message got across to voters: State Senator Obama had stayed in Hawaii, probably lounging on the beach sipping tropical drinks, while a desperately needed anticrime bill went down in defeat in Springfield. Even the *Chicago Tribune,* which favored Obama's candidacy for Congress, scolded that he had chosen "a trip to Hawaii over public safety in Illinois."

At this point Obama knew that his campaign for U.S. congressman had failed. Almost worse, he knew he'd have to go on campaigning, smiling and shaking hands and giving upbeat speeches, as if he thought he were going to win. It was painfully hard. The night of the primary election a couple of months later, he wasn't surprised when he lost to Bobby Rush by thirty-one points.

After this humiliating defeat, Barack Obama spent the next few years working steadily in the state senate. He still had big ambitions about where he could go in politics and what he could accomplish, but he'd learned important lessons. One was about timing—it hadn't been the right time for him to run for Congress, after all. He had to be more patient.

Another lesson Obama learned was about how to campaign. He had a tendency to speak to political audiences the same way he spoke to his University of Chicago classes on constitutional law. Obama was a popular lecturer at the law school, but graduate-level speeches didn't go over as well with the general public. His speeches had to be less intellectual and more about his plans to change voters' lives for the better.

Also, as Jeremiah Wright advised Obama, he had to work harder on building a support network among the people in his party. Obama realized this was true. For instance, Emil Jones, the leader of the Democrats in the state senate, had a great deal of influence. Obama made an effort to get to know Jones and to work with him.

On June 7, 2001, Michelle and Barack's second daughter, Natasha (nicknamed "Sasha"), was born. Now Obama's family needed him more than ever. If he continued to climb the political ladder, he would have less and less time for his personal life. Still, Obama was seriously considering running for U.S. senator in 2004. The Republican senator from Illinois, Peter Fitzgerald, was up for reelection, and he didn't have much support from either his party or his constituents.

When Sasha was just three months old, she came down with meningitis, a sometimes-fatal inflammation of the membrane around the brain and spinal cord. Fortunately, Barack was home at the time. He and Michelle rushed the baby to the hospital and stayed there with her for three days. Barack Obama was a fiercely ambitious, focused, disciplined politician, but in Sasha's hospital room he didn't think about his political future at all.

Shortly after the Obamas' personal crisis, the attacks of September 11, 2001, shook the nation. Barack was in Chicago at the time, and he heard the first reports on his car radio that morning as he drove to a state legislature hearing. Then, with the rest of America, he watched the nightmarish scenes on TV of the hijacked planes crashing into the World Trade Center in New York. He watched the Twin Towers, a symbol of American economic power, crumble, and the Pentagon, the center of American military might, burst into flames. The sights struck fear into all American hearts.

Most state legislators didn't feel called upon to make a public response to the disaster. But Barack Obama was already thinking in wider terms than his state senate district in Illinois. He wrote a thoughtful piece about 9/11, as the event came to be called, for the *Hyde Park Herald*.

Obama noted that the United States needed to increase national security and make sure that al-Qaeda, the terrorist group that had mounted the suicide attacks on the United States, could not launch another attack. But Americans also needed to examine "the sources of such madness," he said. They needed to "devote far more attention to the monumental task of raising the hopes and prospects of embittered children across the globe—children not just in the Middle East, but also in Africa, Asia, Latin America, Eastern Europe and within our own shores."

The aftermath of 9/11 affected not only the United States but also the rest of the world. The stock market plunged. President George W. Bush launched a "War on Terror," beginning with a mission to Afghanistan to hunt down the terrorists. Congress quickly passed a measure to add a new department, Homeland Security, to the federal government.

Among all the far-reaching damage caused by the attacks of 9/11, there was one small coincidence that affected Barack Obama in particular. As a media consultant told him soon after September 11, 2001, the "political dynamics" had changed. Barack Obama the politician had just been hit by some personal bad luck.

What the consultant meant was that the chief of al-Qaeda happened to be named Osama bin Laden. No matter that Barack Obama, American-born, had gotten his name from his Kenyan father, while Osama bin Laden was Saudi Arabian. To most Americans,

"Osama" and "Obama" were both strange, foreign names that sounded almost the same. And "Osama" was a name that called up hate and fear.

Michelle and everyone else, including Shomon, Obama's chief of staff, advised him against entering the Senate race in 2004. But Obama argued that this was his best chance for a political career. If he didn't make his move now, he might as well give up politics and practice law instead.

There was one possible hitch: Democrat Carol Moseley Braun might decide to run. Braun had served as senator from Illinois from 1993 to 1999, the first African American woman to reach the Senate. Now she was thinking of trying to take back her Senate seat. Braun, not only former senator but also former U.S. ambassador to New Zealand, would have been hard for any other Democrat to beat in the primary election. Obama knew she'd have full support from both the black voters and the wealthy white liberals in Chicago.

As Obama waited for Carol Moseley Braun to make up her mind, he promised Michelle that if he ran and lost, he'd forget about politics. He'd concentrate on a career that fit better with their home life and made more money. Money was a big factor, since

Barack Obama's ill-fated campaign for congressman in 2000, although it was underfunded, had cost almost $550,000. Some of that money had come from his own pocket, and the Obamas were still paying off those debts.

Barack suggested to Michelle that if he won the Senate seat, he could write a book and make a lot of money. Michelle, the practical one in their marriage, seriously doubted that—of course he *could* write a book, but most books didn't make money. Look at *Dreams from My Father.* However, by the end of the summer of 2002, Michelle agreed to this one last political campaign.

Part of Obama's motivation for wanting to take part in national politics, and the motivation of people supporting him, was dismay at the political decisions that were now being made in Washington. Throughout the summer and fall of 2002, the Bush administration argued that Saddam Hussein's Iraq possessed weapons of mass destruction, including perhaps nuclear weapons. They also suggested that Iraq had direct links with al-Qaeda, the terrorists who had plotted the 9/11 attacks. President Bush urged Congress to authorize him to use force against Iraq. On October 10 and 11, Congress voted by a wide majority to give the president the power to use force if necessary to disarm Iraq.

Barack Obama thought this measure was a serious mistake, and so did the growing group of antiwar activists in Chicago. They asked him to speak at an antiwar rally in Chicago later in October 2002. Obama worked hard on his speech, carefully spelling out why he opposed invading Iraq. It wasn't because he was against *all* wars, he said. "What I am opposed to is a dumb war."

Obama was skeptical about the Bush administration's evidence that Saddam Hussein possessed weapons of mass destruction. He also thought they were being unrealistic about how easily the war could be won or how much it would cost. He believed they were pursuing the war for political reasons. And he believed the war would increase the instability of the Middle East—and even increase terrorism.

In December 2002, Barack took his family to Hawaii for Christmas as usual. He was still there when he got the news that Carol Moseley Braun had decided to run for president—not senator—in 2004. This was the moment Obama was waiting for.

Chapter 12

Big-Time Politics

In January 2003, Barack Obama announced his candidacy for the U.S. Senate. Several other candidates for the Democratic nomination also declared, but none of them was as formidable an opponent as Carol Moseley Braun would have been.

Obama hired a high-powered staff for his campaign, beginning with media consultant David Axelrod. Axelrod was an experienced and sought-after political consultant, especially gifted at creating TV ads for his clients. He had worked on the U.S. Senate campaigns of Paul Simon of Illinois, Christopher Dodd of Connecticut, and Hillary Clinton of New York, as well as on many others'.

Axelrod could pick and choose the candidates he wanted to work for, so it was telling that he chose newcomer Barack Obama. Obama couldn't afford to pay him as much as some other candidates could, but Axelrod was impressed with Obama's political talent, and he sincerely believed that it was important for Obama to be elected. "I thought that if I could help Barack Obama get to Washington, then I would have accomplished something great in my life," he later told an interviewer. With Axelrod on board, Obama could attract many other top professionals, such as communications director Robert Gibbs, to his campaign.

Obama had important supporters among other politicians, including Emil Jones, the leader of the Democrats in the Illinois state senate. The Reverend Jesse Jackson, Sr., would also use his influence to support Obama. Jackson, the best-known black leader in America, had worked for civil rights ever since the 1960s, and he had twice run for president in the Democratic primaries. His daughter Santita Jackson, a childhood friend of Michelle's, had sung at Michelle and Barack's wedding.

Paul Simon, now a popular former senator, also intended to support Obama. Unfortunately, Simon died suddenly in December 2003, but the fact of his approval helped Obama's candidacy anyway.

At the beginning of his campaign for the U.S. Senate, Obama had to face a hard fact: he was going to need a lot of money. As he explained to a gathering of his financial backers, just to have a good chance of winning the election, he'd need $5 million. But if he could raise $10 million, he guaranteed that he would win.

Not being well-known, Barack Obama didn't have many wealthy donors eager to contribute to his campaign. He had to make phone call after phone call to people who might perhaps be persuaded to contribute, knowing that most of them wouldn't even bother to return his call. The humiliating experience reminded him of when he was living with his grandparents in Hawaii and listening to his grandfather Stanley calling up people to sell them life insurance.

Happily, as the campaign went on, word of mouth began to spread that Obama was an unusually talented and exciting candidate. More people with money came forward to contribute. Also, through appeals on the Internet, Obama gathered numerous smaller donations, and that signaled widespread support for his candidacy. At this time, the idea of raising political funds through the Internet was fairly new.

From the beginning of his campaign, Barack Obama spent nearly every Sunday morning giving talks in black churches around Chicago. He told these audiences that he was a member of Trinity United Church of Christ and that his pastor was the popular preacher Jeremiah Wright. He also filled the congregations in on his background in civil rights: his involvement with the antiapartheid movement, his work as a community organizer in Chicago, and his increasingly impressive record as a state senator.

In 2003 the Democrats gained the majority in the Illinois state senate. That meant that Emil Jones became president of the senate, with the power to assign responsibility for a bill. Working with Jones, Obama sponsored almost eight hundred bills in two years.

More than 280 of these bills became law, and several of them were important gains for civil rights. One law discouraged police from using racial profiling to pull drivers over. Another required the police to videotape prisoners' confessions. Another law expanded the state's health insurance to cover thousands more poor children.

Health insurance was a major issue with Barack Obama, not just for residents of Illinois but also for everyone in the country. It was one of the reasons he was eager to enter the senate, to have a hand in reforming the U.S. health-care system. In November 2003 he was appalled when Congress passed the Medicare Prescription Drug, Improvement, and Modernization Act. He wrote later that this law, supposedly an improvement in the health-care system, "somehow managed to combine the worst aspects of the public and private sectors — price gouging and bureaucratic confusion, gaps in coverage and an eye-popping bill for taxpayers."

Obama also had a strong interest in foreign policy, even aside from the Iraq War. He was very concerned about Sudan, a country in northeastern Africa where a bloody civil war burst out at the beginning of 2003. The Sudanese government, together with the militia, killed hundreds of thousands of people in the Darfur region and made refugees out of millions more. Obama felt that the United States should give more attention to such a massive humanitarian crisis.

As Obama gave speech after speech on the campaign trail, Axelrod counseled him to make his speeches more personal. Obama had a rich baritone voice, like his father, and he was an articulate speaker, but he still had a tendency to get too intellectual. With reminders from Michelle and from his staff, he worked on connecting with his audiences' daily lives.

Since a senatorial race requires many television

appearances in advertisements, interviews, and debates, it was a big advantage that Obama came across well on TV. He had a gift for communicating his sincerity and idealism. He gave an impression of serenity—a deep calm and inner strength—even under the stress of campaigning. When Obama's political consultants conducted a focus-group test, one woman remarked that Obama reminded her of the African American movie star Sidney Poitier.

In his basic campaign speech, Obama started by joking about his name. Everyone knew his name was a disadvantage for a politician, so he brought up the subject himself. People were always getting his last name wrong, he said, garbling it as "Yo mama" or "Alabama." Or they thought it was Irish—O'Bama?

Then he explained that Obama was his Kenyan family name, that "Barack" meant "blessed"—and by the way, his mother was from Kansas. This speech opener gave his audience a quick biography sketch, and it also gained sympathy for him because he was laughing at himself.

David Axelrod produced a series of TV advertisements for Obama, using the theme "Yes, we can." The ads emphasized Obama's Harvard education, which tended to appeal to white voters; his work as a community organizer in Chicago, which tended to appeal to black voters; and his idealism, which appealed to both groups. In the closing, Obama spoke directly to the camera, with quiet conviction. "Now they say we can't change Washington? I'm Barack Obama. I'm running for the United States Senate, and I approve this message to say, 'Yes, we can.'"

When Axelrod first proposed the "Yes, we can" theme, Obama didn't like it. He thought it was too simple. But Michelle thought it was a good slogan for him, so he trusted her judgment. In fact, "Yes, we can" had wide appeal, and the TV ads were very effective.

Meanwhile, Obama's two main Democratic opponents, Dan Hynes and Blair Hull, had spent most of their time attacking each other. As the date of the primary election approached, the polls showed Obama in the lead. Not only that, but it was becoming evident that he had star power. As the *Chicago Sun-Times* put it in a story about personable Chicago politicians, "The first African American president of the *Harvard Law Review* has a movie-star smile and more than a little mystique."

On primary election day in March, Barack Obama voted and then played basketball to relax and take his mind off the campaign. That night, as the results came in, Obama's supporters went wild with delight. He was sweeping the black precincts, but he was also sweeping the precincts that were mainly white. In spite of Chicago's bitter history of racial politics, Obama seemed to be a candidate with universal appeal. And that fact gave people hope for overcoming the bitterness, making Obama all the more attractive.

At Barack Obama's victory party, Michelle, Malia, Sasha, Maya, and Michelle's brother, Craig, joined him onstage. Barack spoke to the overjoyed crowd, and they responded with a chant: "Yes, we can! Yes, we can!"

As the general election campaign began, Obama's Republican rival, Jack Ryan, seemed like a strong opponent. Like Obama, he was young and good-looking, but he also had the personal wealth to spend on a political race. One way Ryan used his money was to hire a cameraman to follow Obama around everywhere he went. The idea was partly to watch for any embarrassing slip Obama might make, and partly to get on his nerves.

The cameraman, sometimes from as close as five feet, filmed Obama's private phone conversations with his wife. He followed him into elevators to film him. He even filmed Obama coming out of the restroom.

Finally Obama turned the tables on Ryan. Leading his cameraman stalker into the press office of the state capitol, he introduced him to a roomful of reporters. The reporters jumped on the story, TV camera crews appeared, and the news story of the day became Ryan unfairly harassing Obama.

But a much more damaging revelation about Jack Ryan was that recently he had gone through a messy divorce from his wife, a Hollywood actress. The media leaped on that story, too, keeping it in the news not only in Illinois but nationwide. By June, Jack Ryan had lost all support, even among Republicans, and he was forced to drop out of the race.

It now seemed certain that Barack Obama would win the general election in November, but the Obama campaign didn't slow down. His staff worked to get him a chance to speak at the Democratic National Convention in Boston at the end of July. As it so happened, the Democratic candidate for president, John Kerry, had met Obama and was impressed with him. Also, the Democratic National Committee wanted to showcase a minority, someone well-spoken, at the convention. In the end, they offered him the keynote speech of the convention.

This was a great opportunity for a state senator,

or even a new U.S. senator. Obama's audience for the keynote speech would be not only the five thousand delegates to the convention but also television viewers across the United States. Depending on how well he spoke, Barack could become a national political star — or a big flop.

Now Obama was in the limelight all the time, and he felt the strain. He was tired but at the same time driven on by nervous energy. His week at the Democratic National Convention began with an appearance on NBC's *Meet the Press*, where he calmly and skillfully answered questions from Tim Russert, a famously tough interviewer. Everywhere he went in the convention center, his staff had to fend off media journalists, photographers, and autograph seekers. In private moments, he worked on his speech.

Obama was a talented writer and speaker in his own right, and he didn't do well if he had to speak someone else's words. So he wrote the speech himself, using input and feedback from his staff and Michelle, as well as some editing from John Kerry's staff.

Tuesday night, just before he was scheduled to go onstage, Barack Obama sat with Michelle for a rare private moment. He wore a dark suit that he'd chosen himself, and the light blue striped tie that his communications director, Gibbs, had been wearing. David Axelrod had thought Obama's own patterned tie was too nondescript and insisted that he change ties with Gibbs. Michelle, who had a strong fashion sense, agreed. It was a small detail, but in this big moment every little detail counted.

Barack had remained amazingly calm up to this point, but now he was nervous. Michelle gave him a hug and teased, "Just don't screw it up, buddy!" It was the right thing to say to break the tension, and they both laughed.

In fact, Barack Obama's speech was an enormous success. The crowd that filled Boston's FleetCenter arena was longing for an uplifting, inspiring speech, and Obama gave it to them. He talked about his family: his Kenyan grandfather, who had big dreams for his goat-herding son; his grandparents from Kansas, who had expected a bright career for their daughter; and his Kenyan father and American mother, who could trust that their mixed-race son, from a family of modest means, would be educated in the best schools in that generous country, America. "This is the true genius of America," he told the audience, "a faith in the simple dreams of the people."

To a country weary of partisan politics, he spoke

of "a belief that we are connected as one people." He asserted, "There's not a liberal America and a conservative America—there's the United States of America. There's not a black America and white America and Latino America and Asian America—there's the United States of America." He spoke of unity, and the "politics of hope" to replace the "politics of cynicism."

The audience responded by jumping to their feet, shouting, and bursting into tears. Veteran TV newsmen like MSNBC's Chris Matthews and CNN's Wolf Blitzer were deeply impressed. As for Michelle, she ran onstage with tears on her face, too, and hugged him again.

Madelyn Dunham, watching her grandson on TV in Hawaii, called him up to say, "You did well." Obama knew that, coming from Toot, that was big praise—she wasn't one to jump up and down or burst into tears. In case she'd praised him too much, she added, "I just kind of worry about you. I hope you keep your head on straight." But later she admitted to a reporter that she thought it was "really quite an exceptional speech."

In spite of Obama's triumph at the Democratic convention, he still had to win the senatorial race in Illinois. The Republicans came up with a new opponent for Obama: Alan Keyes. Keyes was an African American conservative from Maryland. Even the Republican party did not expect Keyes to win the election, and polls soon showed Obama way ahead.

However, Keyes was a fiery speaker, and the Republicans hoped he might burn off a bit of Obama's glow. But although he attacked Obama vigorously, voters didn't pay much attention. In November, Barack Obama won by a landslide.

John Kerry, in contrast, lost the presidential election. President George W. Bush's popularity had dwindled during his first term, but Americans were still worried about the threat of terrorism after the 9/11 attacks. They saw President Bush as more likely to keep America safe than Senator Kerry, who criticized the ongoing Iraq War.

Also, although many Americans were dissatisfied with George W. Bush as the nation's leader, they didn't see Kerry as a better replacement. Kerry, who had been in the Senate since 1984, seemed like an all-too-familiar Washington politician. He didn't have charisma, or the gift of connecting with audiences and inspiring them. John Kerry didn't offer Americans the image of the leader they were looking for.

Chapter 13

Senator Obama

On January 4, 2005, a mild, sunny day in Washington, D.C., Barack Obama was sworn in as a new member of the United States Senate. He was the only African American member of the Senate at this time, and he was only the third African American to be elected to the office since Reconstruction ended in 1877. Michelle, Malia, and Sasha cheered him on from the gallery, and so did Maya, Auma, and Auma's mother, Kezia.

Then Michelle and the girls went back to Chicago, and Barack tried to get used to living on his own in Washington for most of each week. He'd wanted to move the family to Washington, because he knew how much he would miss them, but finally he'd agreed with Michelle that it was better to keep their residence in Chicago, where they had a solid network of family and friends.

The most important person in the Chicago network was Marian Robinson. Michelle's mother loved spending time with Malia and Sasha, and the girls were comfortable and happy with her. Since Marian lived only ten minutes away from the Obamas, she could easily drive the girls to lessons, sports, or friends' houses. Or she could stay overnight with them if Michelle had to be away from home.

Now that the family was in the public eye so much, Michelle felt that they needed a larger home for privacy. In June that year the Obamas bought a stately three-story house, almost a hundred years old, in Hyde Park, not far from the University of Chicago. They could afford to buy a big house because Barack's huge success at the Democratic National Convention had given new life to his book. The paperback publisher of *Dreams from My Father* reissued the book, and it began to sell wildly. The publisher then offered Obama a contract for three more books, with an advance of almost $2 million. Barack's unlikely scheme to solve their financial problems by writing a book had turned out much better than Michelle expected.

Barack rented an apartment in Washington, and he stayed there during the week, when Congress was in session. Weekends he spent in Chicago. He always had official obligations on Saturday, but he saved Sundays for Michelle and their daughters.

At the same time that he was beginning this high-pressure new job, Obama was also writing his next book. The book contract with its large advance had solved the Obamas' money problems, but it only added to the problem of the many demands on his time. Obama titled the new book *The Audacity of Hope*, using a memorable phrase from one of Jeremiah Wright's sermons at Trinity Church.

During his first years in the Senate, Barack Obama worked quietly and tried to keep a low profile. Most of the time, he voted with the rest of the Democrats. An exception was the Military Commissions Act of 2006, which allowed the military to imprison indefinitely, without a hearing, anyone the federal government termed an "unlawful enemy combatant." Obama was one of only thirty-four senators to oppose the act, believing that it violated civil liberties guaranteed by the United States Constitution and encouraged the harsh interrogation of prisoners.

True to his promise to work for unity, against partisan politics, Obama teamed with Republicans on a number of bills. His main accomplishment was a bill he cosponsored with Republican senator Richard

Lugar of Indiana, the respected chairman of the Senate Foreign Relations Committee. Lugar knew that Obama admired the work that he and Senator Sam Nunn had already done on controlling the world's stockpiles of nuclear weapons. He encouraged Obama to join the Foreign Relations Committee and invited him to cosponsor the Lugar-Obama Nonproliferation Initiative, a follow-up to the Nunn-Lugar Cooperative Threat Reduction program.

To gather information for their bill, Obama traveled with Lugar to Russia in 2005. They viewed warehouses full of nuclear missiles, now being closely guarded and dismantled under the Nunn-Lugar program. In neighboring Ukraine, formerly part of the Soviet Union, they saw poorly guarded stores of land mines, as well as of the biological weapon anthrax, and realized how easily terrorists could seize them. The Lugar-Obama Nonproliferation Initiative aimed to reduce worldwide stockpiles of both conventional weapons and weapons of mass destruction. The bill would finally become law in January 2007.

Obama was still traveling with Senator Lugar in Europe on August 29, 2005, when one of the worst natural disasters in U.S. history hit the Gulf Coast. Hurricane Katrina made landfall in Mississippi and

Louisiana, the levees protecting New Orleans failed, and the city was flooded. Almost two thousand people died in the disaster, and tens of thousands lost their homes. The hurricane caused more than $80 billion in damage, making it the costliest natural disaster in U.S. history.

Although the National Hurricane Center and the National Weather Service had given plenty of warning, the city, state, and federal governments were all slow to respond. TV news programs showed shocking scenes of helpless elderly people waiting in wheelchairs in the smothering heat, of bodies floating past flooded neighborhoods, of looters raiding abandoned stores. About twenty thousand refugees huddled in the Louisiana Superdome, the main sports center in New Orleans, without enough food, water, or sanitation.

The Federal Emergency Management Agency (FEMA) was bitterly criticized, and the Bush administration was accused of racism, since the people who suffered most from the effects of the hurricane were poor and black. The hip-hop artist Kanye West said bluntly, "George Bush doesn't care about black people."

Interviewed on ABC's TV program *This Week with George Stephanopoulos*, Obama responded thoughtfully. When he'd returned from Europe, he had visited the

Astrodome in Houston, Texas, where thousands of the refugees were sheltered. He saw that the refugees were like many of the inner-city people he had worked with in Chicago—poor, badly educated, in ill health. They had been barely hanging on, even before the hurricane struck. "We didn't have nothin' before the storm," one woman told him. "Now we got less than nothin'."

It wasn't so much that the federal government was racist, Obama explained to George Stephanopoulos. Instead, it was composed of people who were incompetent and completely out of touch with the way poor people in a city like New Orleans actually lived. He thought that "whoever was in charge of planning was so detached from the realities of inner-city life in a place like New Orleans that they couldn't conceive of the notion that somebody couldn't load up their SUV, put one hundred dollars' worth of gas in there, put [in] some sparkling water, and drive off to a hotel and check in with a credit card."

In August 2006 Senator Obama took an official trip to Africa as a congressional delegation. He had planned this trip since the beginning of 2005. It would be a fact-finding mission about the AIDS epidemic in many African countries and the gross human rights violations in Darfur.

The first country on Obama's route was South Africa. Near Cape Town, he toured the prison where Nelson Mandela, hero of the antiapartheid resistance, had been held for eighteen of his twenty-seven years of imprisonment. This was a moving moment for Obama, who had first been drawn into politics over the issue of apartheid in South Africa.

The next day he visited a health center in a shantytown area outside Cape Town. There he spoke to reporters about the acute epidemic of AIDS, one of the worst in the world, from which South Africans were suffering. The president of South Africa, Thabo Mbeki, had doubted in a public statement that the disease of AIDS was caused by the HIV infection, although this was an established medical fact.

Obama hoped to meet with Mbeki during his visit, and he didn't want to offend him. But he felt that AIDS was too grave a threat to be polite about. He criticized Mbeki's government sharply as being "in denial" of scientific facts about AIDS, and he called for a "sense of urgency." The next day, Mbeki refused to meet with Obama. However, many other South Africans were grateful to him for speaking out.

After four days in South Africa, Obama flew to Kenya. Michelle, Malia, and Sasha joined him for this part of the trip. So did his half sister Auma, who was now living near London and working in social services. Barack was eager to show his children the country of their grandfather Obama and introduce them to their Kenyan relatives. Obama also hoped, as he explained at a news conference in Nairobi, to be "a bridge between the two nations" with this official trip to Kenya.

As it soon became apparent, the media attention during the visit was so intense that the Obamas had almost no personal time. Also, everywhere Barack Obama went in Kenya, he was greeted by adoring crowds. To Kenyans, he was an American prince. In Nairobi a young man in the crowd held aloft an oil portrait of Obama that he had painted. Obama in the picture had a glow around him, almost as if he were a saint.

Obama and his family made the trip from Nairobi to his father's childhood home in Kolego, as Obama had done in 1988 and 1991. The difference was that the first two trips had been private, but this one was overwhelmingly public. Instead of traveling with Auma by bus with chickens on his lap, as he had in 1988, Obama flew from Nairobi followed by a huge press corps.

As the centerpiece of their visit to Obama's ancestral home, Barack and Michelle planned to have their blood tested for AIDS at a provincial medical clinic. They wanted to make the point that anyone could—and should—get tested for AIDS. Thousands of Kenyans crowded the streets on the way to the clinic, dancing and chanting, "Everything is possible with Obama." Camera crews and reporters struggled through the cheering throngs to watch the test in a trailer provided by the U.S. Centers for Disease Control and Prevention (CDC). The CDC estimated that half a million more people might have themselves tested, just as a result of the Obamas' demonstration.

Next Obama and his family visited a CARE Kenya project far out in the bush. This project was also connected with the AIDS crisis, enabling older women to support children orphaned by AIDS. Obama himself had provided part of the funding for the project, which gave money to the women to invest in equipment such as sewing machines.

At the gathering of the women and children involved in the CARE project, Obama was honored with worshipful dancing and singing. Michelle said to a reporter, "It's all a bit overwhelming." The intense attention and adulation continued to be overwhelming as the Obamas proceeded to a school in Kogelo, the village near his family compound. Obama had donated money to the school, and it was named after him: the Senator Obama Kogelo Secondary School. Thousands of Luo tribespeople had gathered here for a combined celebration of Obama's visit and a political rally for the upcoming Kenyan elections.

After ceremonies at the school, the Obamas then drove the short distance to the Obama family compound, where Barack's Kenyan grandmother, Granny, greeted them. She was now eighty-three. Barack had planned that he and Michelle and their daughters would spend more than two hours in private with her. But because of the crowds and the reporters and cameras waiting, they had only forty minutes, barely enough time to eat a meal together.

At the end of their Kenya visit, the Obamas took two days to enjoy a safari in Masai country. Then Barack and Michelle flew northwest to Chad, where they visited a refugee camp filled with victims of the civil war in neighboring Sudan. Obama had planned to visit Darfur itself, but the Sudanese government refused to let him into the country. More than 200,000 refugees from Darfur lived in camps like this in the desert, surviving on rations and water trucked in by the UN.

By visiting the camp and talking with some of the refugees, Obama hoped to learn more about Darfur. But the visit was frustrating, because he had less than two hours to listen to the refugees, and their stories had to be translated from Arabic to French to English for him. However, he hoped that his appearance would draw more media attention to the plight of the refugees.

In October 2006, soon after Barack Obama returned from Africa, his new book was published. *The Audacity of Hope: Thoughts on Reclaiming the American Dream* was an immediate success. It wasn't as personal a book as *Dreams from My Father,* but it was still much more straightforward and readable than the usual politician's book. It expressed, in more detail, the themes of his speech at the Democratic National Convention in 2004: We are one nation. Our best comes out in working together for the common good. Everyone deserves a fair chance at the American dream.

In *The Audacity of Hope,* Obama sharply criticized many of the policies of the Bush administration, especially the Iraq War. Obama had opposed the war as long ago as the fall of 2002, before the war was even officially launched. Now he pointed out that the Iraq War was only one example of the Bush administration's confused foreign policy. For example, why invade Iraq but not North Korea? Kim Jong Il's government was just as repressive as Saddam Hussein's, and North Korea actually possessed weapons of mass destruction.

At the same time, Obama was careful to make the point that he didn't consider George W. Bush to be a bad man. In fact, he assumed that President Bush and the people in his administration were sincerely trying to do what they thought best for the country. In one-to-one meetings with Bush, Obama found the president friendly and likeable.

The Audacity of Hope also communicated Barack Obama's ability to laugh at himself. For example, he told about calling Michelle from Washington to bring her up-to-date about how his bill with Dick Lugar was going. Caught up in the work of the Senate, Barack couldn't imagine anything more important than the Nonproliferation Initiative.

But Michelle was on a different track, on which the most important issue was an ant invasion of their house. She interrupted him with a request: Would he pick up some ant traps on his way home from Washington the next day? Bemused, Barack wondered whether famous senators like Edward Kennedy or

John McCain ever had to buy ant traps after negotiating legislation of worldwide significance in the
Senate. He could count on Michelle to bring him
down to earth.

Obama wasn't up for reelection in 2006, since U.S.
senators have six-year terms. But he helped other
Democratic candidates campaign. To his satisfaction,
the national elections in November gave the Democrats a majority in both the Senate and the House of
Representatives. That, together with President Bush's
continuing unpopularity, boded well for the Democrats to capture the White House in 2008.

Chapter 14

Running for President

During the fall of 2006, Barack Obama turned to the question of whether he should try to run for president in 2008. Although the election was more than two years away, he needed to decide now. A presidential campaign would require an enormous effort, far beyond what he and his supporters had done for his Senate race.

Obama consulted first with Michelle and with his most trusted staff, David Axelrod and Robert Gibbs. Then he went on to talk with a range of friends whose opinions he respected, including the Reverends Jeremiah Wright and Jesse Jackson. The feedback he got was very positive.

Although Barack Obama was young for the presidency—he will be forty-seven in January 2009—he wasn't as young as Theodore Roosevelt, the youngest president at forty-two upon inauguration. John F. Kennedy had become president at forty-three. Obama lacked experience at the national level of government, but JFK had served only two terms in the Senate. Abraham Lincoln had served only *one* term as congressman from Illinois before his election to the presidency.

One encouraging sign for Obama's candidacy was that his new book, *The Audacity of Hope,* was a runaway bestseller. This success gave him a great deal of good publicity. His face was on the cover of *Time* magazine, and his book tour included an appearance with Michelle on *Oprah*.

President George W. Bush's unpopularity was an advantage for any Democratic candidate. Bush himself wouldn't be able to run, since 2008 would be the end of his second four-year term. But the Republican candidate would have to struggle to avoid being linked with the problems of the Bush administration: the seemingly endless war in Iraq, the soaring national budget deficit, the sluggish economy.

In considering whether Barack should run for president, Michelle worried about the effects of his political career on their family. A presidential bid meant that Michelle, as well as Barack, had to spend the next two years campaigning. It meant even less privacy and time with each other and with their two young children.

Still, by December 2006, Michelle had agreed to support Barack in his bid for the presidency. She made him promise to stop smoking, however, before she promised to help him campaign. Also, she was determined to keep her children's lives stable, in spite of the tremendous pressures of their father's run for president.

To free up time for campaigning, Michelle quit her position on the board of TreeHouse, a supplier to Wal-Mart Stores. She also cut back on her work as vice president at the University of Chicago Hospitals. And Marian Robinson, Michelle's mother, quit her job as a bank secretary. Now she could be available full-time for Malia and Sasha when Michelle and Barack were on the road.

As Obama prepared to begin his campaign for president, he received some bad publicity. Antoin "Tony" Rezko, a friend, fund-raiser, and heavy contributor to Obama's campaign for the Senate, was indicted for fraud in October 2006. (In June 2008 Rezko was convicted on sixteen counts of corruption.) In November 2006 it came out that in June 2005, at the same time that the Obamas bought their house in

South Chicago, the Rezkos had bought the lot next door. Obama then bought a piece of Rezko's property to add to his yard, so that his children would have more room to play.

Obama hadn't done anything illegal or violated the Senate's ethics rules, but he admitted that he'd created the *appearance* that Rezko was doing him a favor by selling him part of his lot. This was a mistake, Obama said—"boneheaded," in fact. But if there had to be an embarrassing revelation, it was better to get it out of the way early in the campaign.

In February 2007 Barack Obama announced his candidacy for president of the United States. He made his announcement outside the Old State Capitol in Springfield, Illinois. "It's a little chilly today," he joked. (It was 12 degrees F.) "But I'm fired up." The cheering, beaming crowd of 15,000 was clearly fired up, too. As Obama reminded the audience, this site was where Abraham Lincoln had made his famous speech using the well-known quotation from the Bible: "A house divided against itself cannot stand."

Barack Obama was a bright new political star, and many commentators compared him with John F. Kennedy, also a handsome, inspiring young senator when he ran for president. But throughout 2007 the front-runner for the Democratic nomination was Senator Hillary Clinton of New York. As former First Lady for eight years during Bill Clinton's administration, she was much better known than Obama. Also, she had a powerful political organization in place and the resources of her husband's backers.

However, Barack Obama's campaign quickly set a record for fund-raising, bringing in $58 million in the first half of 2007. An impressive number of the donations were from small donors, giving less than $200 each. Much of this money was raised through the Internet, since Obama's young campaign staffers were familiar with the Internet and knew how to use it. Through the Internet they were also able to quickly recruit and organize an army of volunteers.

Spontaneous Obama-supporting groups sprang up on social networking sites such as Facebook. By March 2007 there were more than five hundred Obama groups on Facebook. One of them, Students for Barack Obama, grew into a political action committee with almost 62,000 members.

Barack Obama's fame was also spread through an independently produced Internet video, "I Got a Crush . . . on Obama," first appearing on YouTube in June 2007. It was a comedic video making fun of how Obama's supporters swooned over him. It featured a young woman posing and singing provocatively against a background of Obama photos. This video was quickly viewed by millions of Americans and shown in TV news broadcasts. However, Obama wasn't pleased about the free publicity, because the video had upset Malia and Sasha. "You do wish people would think about what impact their actions have on kids and families," he said.

Michelle Obama campaigned vigorously for her husband, both in joint appearances and by herself. But the Obamas tried to keep their children's lives as normal as possible. Most of the time, Malia and Sasha stayed home in Chicago. "Our kids thrive on stability and routine and consistency," Michelle explained in an interview. Even during the summer of 2007, when the girls were out of school, Michelle planned their campaign trips around birthday parties and day-camp field trips.

Barack's American sister, Maya Soetoro-Ng, also campaigned for him, taking two months off from work. Even his grandmother Madelyn Dunham, although she was eighty-six and frail, took part in a TV advertisement for Obama.

As the primary election season opened in January

2008, Barack Obama began to draw even with Hillary Clinton. First he won the Iowa caucus. In the New Hampshire primary, although Clinton won the most votes, they won the same number of delegates to the Democratic National Convention. Obama congratulated Hillary Clinton on election night after the votes were in, but his speech to his supporters sounded more like a victory speech than a concession. He used again the slogan that had been so successful in his campaign for the U.S. Senate: "Yes, we can." His audience roared back, "Yes—we—can!"

Obama went on to win the primaries in Nevada and South Carolina. On February 5, called Super Tuesday because so many states held their primary elections that day, Obama won twenty more delegates than Clinton. (By this time the Democratic candidate in third place, John Edwards, had dropped out of the race.) In a televised speech that night, even before all the returns were in, Obama talked about what he would do as president:

> I'll be a president who finally brings Democrats and Republicans together to make health care affordable and available for every single American. We will put a college education

within reach of anyone who wants to go, and instead of just talking about how great our teachers are, we will reward them for their greatness, with more pay and better support. And we will harness the ingenuity of farmers and scientists and entrepreneurs to free this nation from the tyranny of oil once and for all.

One clear advantage Barack Obama had over Hillary Clinton, as far as most Democrats were concerned, was that he had opposed the Iraq War from the beginning. His speech of October 2002, calling it a "dumb war," had been widely distributed over the Internet. When Hillary Clinton tried to paint him as inexperienced, Obama could reply that good judgment was more important than many years of experience. In October 2002, Clinton had voted along with most of Congress to give President Bush the authority to attack Iraq.

In March, Barack Obama was hit with some bad publicity in connection with the Reverend Jeremiah Wright. Besides being Obama's friend and pastor for twenty years, Wright had a small role in Obama's campaign as one of more than 170 people on Obama's African American Religious Leadership Committee.

Now ABC News was broadcasting video clips of Wright's fiery sermons in which he had sharply criticized the United States for its racism. He had also said the United States had brought the disaster of September 11, 2001, on itself through its own "terrorism."

Most Americans were shocked and outraged by Wright's words, and they wondered how Barack Obama could be so close to Wright. Obama asked Wright to drop his association with the campaign, since his presence could only hurt the candidate now. Obama also told the media that he strongly condemned Wright's inflammatory statements. But he didn't repudiate Wright. He felt that would be disloyal to the minister who had baptized him when he joined the church, married him and Michelle, and baptized their children.

The incident convinced Obama that he needed to talk openly to Americans, white and black, about the issue of race relations in the United States. He wrote a speech entitled "A More Perfect Union," a phrase from the preamble to the U.S. Constitution. To underline his belief that the fundamental principles of the nation were at stake, he gave the speech at the National Constitution Center in Philadelphia.

Obama said afterward that he was "channeling

my mother" as he wrote the speech. He remembered
her positive, practical approach to racial differences,
and how disturbed she'd been by the anger that the
black leader Malcolm X expressed in the 1960s. Perhaps he also remembered the story of the time his
father won over the white man in the bar at Waikiki
by talking to him about race in a straightforward,
confident way.

Most media commentators and politicians, Republican as well as Democratic, praised Obama's courage
in addressing the racial issue, and felt that he handled
it well. Chris Matthews of MSNBC said Obama
had given "what many of us think is one of the great
speeches in American history." However, in the short
run the uproar over Wright caused Obama's favorabil-
ity in the polls to drop from 50 percent to 45 percent.

That might have been the end of the incident,
except that in April, Jeremiah Wright appeared before
the National Press Club and repeated his controversial views. Worse, he suggested that Obama secretly
agreed with him. At this point Barack Obama finally
felt forced to disown his former friend and pastor. In
May, the Obamas reluctantly left Trinity Church.

In early March, in the Republican primaries,
Senator John McCain had become the presumptive

nominee—meaning that the party would formally nominate him during their national convention in September. McCain could afford to relax a bit and gather his forces for the general election, while Barack Obama and Hillary Clinton kept up a fierce struggle for the Democratic nomination through March, April, and May. But Obama gradually outdistanced Clinton.

On June 3, when all the primary results were in, Obama had enough delegates to win the Democratic nomination. He was now the presumptive nominee of the Democratic Party. On June 7, Clinton announced that she was endorsing Obama.

For the general election, Obama would need more money. In 2004 both George W. Bush's campaign and John Kerry's campaign had raised well over $200 million. Some political observers predicted that each major candidate in the 2008 election would have to raise more than $400 million.

In mid-June, Obama decided to turn down public financing for the general election. Public financing would provide $84 million, but then the candidate had to accept strict spending limits. Obama was confident that he could raise much more than $84 million, since he'd raised $55 million in February alone. This was a new record for fund-raising in one month. In order to challenge John McCain in traditionally Republican states, he would need large amounts of money, and he would need freedom from spending limits.

In June alone, the Obama campaign raised $52 million, more than twice the amount raised by John McCain. Senator McCain had accepted public funding for the general election, and his campaign criticized Obama loudly for failing to "stand on principle and keep his word to the American people." This was a reminder that Obama had originally agreed to limit himself to public funding if his Republican opponent did the same.

During this year of nonstop campaigning, Barack Obama tried to weave his family life in with his hectic schedule. Since Barack was scheduled to give an Independence Day speech in Butte, Montana, Michelle decided that the Obamas would celebrate Malia's birthday while watching the Fourth of July parade there. So Barack gave his speech, and the Obamas hosted a picnic in Butte for family and friends. Malia would have a private birthday party with her friends the week after her actual birthday.

Also on Barack and Michelle's schedule during the Fourth of July celebration was an interview for the program *Access Hollywood*. They hadn't planned to include Malia and Sasha in the interview, but Barack and Michelle were in a relaxed mood that day and thought it might be fun. The interviewer was surprised and delighted to include the girls at the last minute.

Malia told the interviewer how her father had embarrassed her once by shaking hands with one of her nine-year-old friends, as if she were a voter. "You don't really shake hands with kids," explained Malia. Sasha confided that everyone in the family except her father liked ice cream. She and Malia agreed that their parents were most likely to get mad at them for whining. They also agreed that they liked to see their parents holding hands or kissing.

In all, the interview didn't reveal anything very private, and Michelle and the children didn't seem uncomfortable about it. But Barack said afterward that it was a mistake. "I don't think it's healthy and it's something that we'll be avoiding in the future," he said. His family life was very precious to him, and this felt a little too intrusive.

Ever since Barack Obama emerged as the likely Democratic candidate, Senator McCain had been attacking him for his lack of foreign policy experience. McCain had strongly supported the Iraq War from the beginning, and he tried to cast Obama as

naïve and ignorant of military matters. McCain kept
challenging Obama to travel to Iraq and see for himself how well the war was going.

Obama saw this challenge as an opportunity, and
he was glad to take McCain up on it. By meeting with
world leaders and visiting troubled parts of the world,
he could demonstrate to American voters that he had
a statesmanlike presence. He could discuss his views
about various important decisions he would have to
make if he won the election. So later in July, Obama
left for the Middle East and western Europe.

Obama asked Senators Chuck Hagel of Nebraska
and Jack Reed of Rhode Island to travel to Iraq
with him. Hagel, though Republican, had criticized
the Bush administration repeatedly for its conduct of
the Iraq War. Also, as a member of the Senate Foreign Relations Committee, Hagel had experience that
Obama lacked. Reed, a Democrat, was a member of
the important Senate Armed Forces Committee. Reed
had been in Congress since 1990, and Hagel since
1996.

One of the highlights of Obama's trip abroad
was his stop in Berlin, Germany. There, at the Berlin
Wall that had once separated Soviet-dominated East
Germany from West Germany, he spoke to a crowd

of 200,000, many of them waving American flags. Viewers remembered that President John F. Kennedy and President Ronald Reagan had also made memorable speeches in Berlin. If McCain intended to make his rival look presidential, he had succeeded.

Chapter 15

President Barack Obama

The Democratic National Convention of 2008 was held at the end of August in Denver, Colorado. It had already been decided that the convention would nominate Barack Obama for president. But it was vital for the Democrats to heal the split between the Obama camp and the Clinton camp. Many supporters of Hillary Clinton were bitterly disappointed, and some of them even threatened to vote for Republican John McCain.

Just before the convention began, Barack Obama announced his choice for vice president: Senator Joe Biden of Delaware. Senator Biden had served in the Senate since 1973, and he had extensive experience in foreign policy, which Obama lacked.

On August 25, the first day of the convention, Michelle Obama gave the headline prime-time speech. Republicans had often tried to portray her as a tough, almost radical woman—not the kind of person Americans would want as First Lady. Michelle took this chance to emphasize her traditional values and devotion to her family.

The following night Senator Hillary Clinton gave the headline prime-time speech, directing it chiefly to her supporters. She thanked them for fighting for her, but urged them to work just as hard for Barack Obama. In a pointed rejection of the idea that Clinton backers might now swing to Senator McCain, she said with great emphasis, "No how. No way. No McCain."

The following day, Senator Clinton called for suspending the roll call of delegates and nominating Barack Obama by acclamation. That night, former president Bill Clinton further reinforced party unity by declaring, "Barack Obama is ready to be president of the United States."

For Barack Obama's acceptance speech on August 28, the convention moved to Invesco Field at Mile High Stadium in Denver. Nearly 80,000 people packed the stadium, and 38 million Americans watched the televised event. Speaking on the theme "Change You Can Believe In," Obama inspired the audience with hope for the future. "I will restore our moral standing," he promised, "so that America is once again that last, best hope for all who are called to the cause of freedom, who long for lives of peace, and who yearn for a better future."

With the success of the convention, Obama's numbers rose in the polls. However, the very next day John McCain grabbed the nation's attention by announcing his choice for vice president. To the surprise of almost everyone, he picked Governor Sarah Palin of Alaska, who had no national political experience.

At the Republican National Convention in St. Paul, Minnesota, the following week, Republicans responded to Sarah Palin with enthusiasm. They liked her cheerfully feisty style, her working-class background, and her conservative beliefs. They were hopeful that many independent voters who had supported Senator Clinton would now be drawn to Governor Palin. Coming out of the convention, the Republicans had renewed energy and a larger bump in the polls than expected.

Some Democrats were seriously worried that McCain might have gained a permanent advantage by choosing Palin. They begged Barack Obama to get angry at accusations from the McCain campaign they felt were unfair and to go on the attack. However, Obama refused to get rattled.

Meanwhile, the U.S. economy was shaken by the

worst financial crisis since the Wall Street Crash in 1929, which had set off the Great Depression. The crisis had been building since 2007, when the housing bubble burst. The prices of private homes, which had been rising steadily for a number of years, fell sharply. Homeowners who had taken out large mortgages, expecting their houses to increase in value, were left with property worth less than the loans they had to pay back. Many of them simply could not make their payments, and hundreds of thousands of families faced losing their homes through foreclosure.

To make matters worse, many lenders had given mortgages to buyers who obviously could not afford them. These lenders had quickly sold the risky loans to investors, who now held worthless stock. During 2008, it came out that even respected and apparently solid financial institutions had invested heavily in the unsound mortgages.

The nation was shocked as some of the largest investment banks, including Bear Stearns and Lehman Brothers, collapsed. In rapid succession, other major financial institutions either went bankrupt or had to be bailed out by the federal government. In September, the government took over Fannie Mae and Freddie Mac, the largest mortgage-backing enterprises in the

United States. Likewise, the government also took over the failing American International Group (AIG), an insurance giant.

On September 19, Secretary of the Treasury Henry M. Paulson, Jr., speaking for the Bush administration, announced a rescue plan for the nation's entire financial system. Paulson asked Congress for the authority to buy up the unsound mortgage-backed securities that had caused the panic—as much as $700 billion worth.

The panic on the stock market was calmed for the moment by the news of a plan, but Congress was thrown into turmoil. Ordinary American citizens on "Main Street," struggling with rising prices, unemployment, and lack of health insurance, were outraged. As they told their representatives and senators, they did not want to bail out the "fat cats" on Wall Street who had invested recklessly and raked in big profits.

However, over the next week it became clear that the collapse of the U.S. banking system would cause disaster to ordinary Americans too. If banks failed, businesses would no longer be able to get the credit they needed to operate, and their employees would lose their jobs. Individuals would not be able to get loans to buy a car or send a child to college. The nation's economy would grind almost to a halt, as it had during the Great Depression.

Congress discussed frantically how to act on Paulson's proposal. John McCain announced that he was suspending his campaign until the financial crisis was solved. He called for the first presidential debate, scheduled for September 26, to be postponed.

Remaining calm, Barack Obama consulted with a group of economic experts, conservative as well as liberal. He had believed for some time that speculation in the home mortgage market was a serious threat to the nation's economic health.

On September 26, although Congress was still working out an agreement, Senator McCain flew from Washington to Mississippi for the presidential debate. The location, the University of Mississippi in Oxford, underlined the historic significance of Barack Obama's candidacy. The university, known as "Ole Miss," had been the scene of race riots in 1962, when the first black student, James Meredith, attempted to enroll.

During the debate John McCain tried to cast Barack Obama as inexperienced and naïve about foreign policy and military issues. Obama repeatedly linked McCain to the failures of the eight-year Bush administration. Obama also pointed out that Senator

McCain, in spite of his years of experience, had been wrong on several crucial issues. Obama reminded the audience that the war in Iraq, which Senator McCain had predicted would be won easily, was draining $10 billion per month from the U.S. Treasury.

Obama also emphasized that Senator McCain had supported President Bush's economic policies, including the decision to loosen government regulation of banks. Obama quoted McCain as declaring recently that "the fundamentals of our economy are strong." Given the desperate condition of the U.S. economy, that made McCain seem hopelessly out of touch.

While neither man clearly won or lost the debate, polls a week later showed that Obama was in the lead again. Voters saw him as more capable than McCain of handling the financial crisis, which was their top concern. And some of the enthusiasm for McCain's running mate, Sarah Palin, had worn off.

On September 29, the House of Representatives defeated a measure based on the Bush administration's plan for rescuing the financial system. The Dow Jones industrial average, a main indicator of the stock market, promptly dropped more than 770 points, its biggest one-day loss ever. It was obvious that Congress had to act, no matter how unpopular the rescue measure was with their constituents. On October 3, the House passed a revised version of the bill, already approved by the Senate.

With up to $700 billion now committed to the financial rescue plan, Barack Obama knew as president he would not be able to accomplish all the goals that he envisioned. Still, Obama was determined to give tax relief to middle-class and working-class citizens, and to reform the health care system so that all Americans had adequate health care. He was also resolved to invest in programs that would create thousands of jobs at the same time that they benefited the country in other ways. One was an energy program for developing renewable sources of energy and ending dependence on foreign oil. Another was a plan to repair the nation's run-down roadways and bridges.

The second presidential debate took place on October 7 at Belmont University in Nashville, Tennessee. The format of this debate was town-hall style. More than eighty undecided voters shared the stage with the two candidates and the moderator. Barack Obama and John McCain answered questions from the undecided voters, as well as questions sent in by e-mail. Most of the questions dealt with the faltering economy, which had lost 159,000 jobs in September.

In a poll taken immediately after the debate, voters' opinion of McCain didn't change, but their opinion of Obama rose by a few points. Republican as well as Democratic commentators agreed that Obama had won the debate by a slight margin. But the race was still too close to call. The third and last debate was held on October 15, at Hofstra University in Hempstead, New York.

During the third debate Senator McCain attacked Obama more vigorously, but Obama remained calm and cool. He kept the focus on the faltering national economy, which he blamed on the Bush administration's policies, and repeated his claim that a McCain presidency would be like having four more years of George W. Bush. The economy was still by far the main issue for voters, and it appeared they had more confidence in Obama's ability to lead the country out of the economic crisis. National polls showed Obama ahead. In the final week, Obama's lead narrowed, but most national polls still put him ahead.

In the last stretch of the campaign, many moderate Republicans came out in support of Barack Obama. Colin Powell, the greatly respected former general and former secretary of state in the Bush administration, endorsed Obama. So did former Massachusetts governor William Weld.

This had been a watershed race for the presidency in several ways. For one thing, Hillary Clinton was the first woman to come so close to winning a major party nomination. Sarah Palin was the first woman to be nominated for vice president by the Republican party. John McCain, if he had won the election, would have been the oldest president to begin a first term. But most striking, Barack Obama was the first African American candidate nominated by a major party. If he won, it would signal an important change in Americans' attitudes toward race.

The presidential contest of 2008 had been the longest as well as the most expensive campaign in U.S. history, costing more than $1 billion total. The McCain campaign spent $176 million just on television advertising, while the Obama campaign spent $278 million. The Obama campaign had received a record number of more than three million donations, large and small; Obama could afford to advertise even in states where he wasn't likely to win, such as Senator McCain's home state of Arizona. Besides money, Obama had the advantage of a huge army of volunteers to go door to door in the battleground states, such as Ohio, to get out the vote.

Although both McCain and Obama had set out to wage positive campaigns, the election turned negative in the final weeks. Senator McCain had told his team not to bring up the subject of Obama's former pastor, the controversial Jeremiah Wright. However, at the end of October the National Republican Trust PAC ran television advertisements in Ohio, Pennsylvania, and Florida reminding voters of Obama's close association with Wright. As for the Obama team, they gleefully publicized Vice President Richard Cheney's endorsement of John McCain. They had worked for many months to link Senator McCain with the unpopular Bush administration, and Vice President Cheney was even less popular than the president.

The presidential election of 2008 promised to be a record-setter for voter turnout. Since a low in the election of 1996, the turnout for presidential elections had been slowly rising. In 2008, both Democrats and Republicans made extra efforts to register voters and get them to the polls. There were predictions that the turnout would top the 63.1 percent of 1960, when John F. Kennedy won the presidency. It might even match the 66 percent of a century ago in 1908, when William Howard Taft was elected president. The Democrats had registered an unusually large number of new black, Hispanic, and young voters, groups with typically low turnout rates. All these groups tended to favor Barack Obama.

During the hectic last weeks of the campaign, Barack Obama took a trip to Hawaii. His grandmother Madelyn Dunham, eighty-six, was gravely ill, and it was not certain that she would live even until Election Day. However, she was mentally alert, and Obama was glad he could spend time at her bedside, talking with her. Michelle, campaigning in place of her husband, told the audience what Barack's grandmother had meant to him. "She taught him with her quiet confidence and love and support that he could do anything."

Barack's sister Maya was with their grandmother when she died on November 3. Although it was sad that Madelyn Dunham hadn't lived long enough to see her grandson elected president, she had been able to vote for him by absentee ballot. And by the day before the election, it seemed probable that Obama would be the winner.

Obama had held up well under the long, high-pressure campaign, although he looked older than he had when it had begun almost two years before. There was gray in his hair, and he had lost some weight. But he was steadier and more confident than ever. His steadiness was reflected in the tireless, well-organized work of his campaign, and his calm, resolute manner had convinced voters that Obama had the right temperament for the stressful job of president of the United States. On Wednesday, October 29, more than 33 million viewers watched a thirty-minute "infomercial" aired during prime time on the major networks by the Obama campaign. The advertisement combined images from the campaign trail with clips of Barack Obama addressing voters, as well as of ordinary Americans telling about their difficulties in these hard economic times.

On November 3, Barack Obama made a last push to win the battleground states. He began the day with a rally in Jacksonville, Florida. He traveled on to rallies in North Carolina and Virginia. If Barack Obama won all the states the polls showed as leaning Democratic, as well as the solidly Democratic states, he would have 291 electoral votes—more than the 270 he needed to win. But he and his followers were not going to relax at this point. They aimed for a wide margin of victory, which would help unite the country behind the new president.

On the evening of November 3, Obama appeared in a prerecorded interview on the TV program *Monday Night Football*. Asked about the best advice he'd ever gotten from the sports world, Obama remembered the words of his high school basketball coach, who told him, "This is not about you. It's about the team." Obama gave a related answer to another question: What personality quality of his did he want voters to think about as they went to the polls? He said, "That I'm going to fight for them."

On November 4, Election Day, Barack and Michelle Obama, accompanied by Malia and Sasha, voted at a neighborhood elementary school. The girls hoped their father would win, of course. But in any case, they were happy the long campaign was almost over. Their parents had promised them a puppy after the election. Afterward, Barack was off to Indianapolis for a final campaign stop.

That afternoon, Obama returned to Chicago to await the election returns. He followed his Election Day tradition of playing basketball with friends, then ate dinner at home with his family. His election night rally was scheduled to begin at eight thirty Central time at Grant Park in Chicago, a site which could hold hundreds of thousands of people. Everyone at the rally would have to stand for several hours.

Polling officials had been worried that the large turnout would cause problems at voting sites, and in some places voters did have to wait in line for hours. But this year many more voters—almost a third—cast their votes early, as most states allowed early or no-excuse absentee ballot voting. Apparently the unusual number of early voters helped prevent congestion at the polls on Election Day itself.

The TV networks were cautious about calling the election too early, because in 2004 some of them had mistakenly reported John Kerry in the lead, based on unreliable exit polls. This year, they agreed not to call the results for a state until all the votes for that state were in.

As polls in the Eastern time zone began to close, the country watched especially for results from the contested states of Indiana, Virginia, North Carolina, Florida, and New Hampshire. If Obama won these, it would be a clear signal that the election was going his way.

Pennsylvania was also important, because John McCain had fought long and hard to win this Democratic-leaning state. If he did win Pennsylvania, it would be an encouraging sign that he might win the election after all. But Pennsylvania went for Obama. Ohio, too, was a key battleground state. No Republican in modern times had won the presidency without Ohio—and Ohio went for Barack Obama.

Before eleven p.m. Eastern time, it was clear that Obama would also win Virginia. At eleven, when the polls closed on the West Coast and Obama carried California, Washington, and Oregon, most of the networks pronounced Barack Obama the winner. The final results would not be reported until the following day, but already Obama had more than 300 electoral votes. It would be a sweeping victory. John McCain called Obama from Phoenix, Arizona, to concede the election.

All across the country, the rallies for Obama turned into celebration parties. At midnight, Barack Obama appeared on the stage in front of the enormous crowd at Grant Park to give his victory speech. Thanking all his supporters, he told them that the victory truly belonged to them, rather than him. He called for all Americans to unite to solve the serious problems facing the country.

President-elect Obama told an inspiring story of one voter in Atlanta: Ann Nixon Cooper, an African American woman who was 106 years old. "She was born just a generation past slavery; a time when there were no cars on the road or planes in the sky; when someone like her couldn't vote for two reasons—because she was a woman and because of the color of her skin.

"And tonight, I think about all that she's seen throughout her century in America—the heartache and the hope; the struggle and the progress; the times we were told that we can't, and the people who pressed on with that American creed: Yes, we can."

As Barack Obama continued his speech, he repeated again and again the phrase that had been the rallying cry of his campaign: "Yes, we can." And his audience, waving a sea of American flags, repeated solemnly, many with tears in their eyes, "Yes, we can."

"America," Obama finished, "we have come so far. We have seen so much. But there is so much more to do. So tonight, let us ask ourselves: If our children should live to see the next century—if my daughters should be so lucky to live as long as Ann Nixon Cooper—what change will they see? What progress will we have made?

"This is our chance to answer that call. This is our moment. This is our time—to put our people back to work and open doors of opportunity for our kids; to restore prosperity and promote the cause of peace; to reclaim the American Dream and reaffirm that fundamental truth—that out of many, we are one; that while we breathe, we hope; and where we are met with cynicism, and doubt, and those who tell us that we can't, we will respond with that timeless creed that sums up the spirit of a people: Yes, we can."

Sources

Books

Mendell, David. *Obama: From Promise to Power*. New York: HarperCollins, 2007.

Obama, Barack. *The Audacity of Hope: Thoughts on Reclaiming the American Dream*. New York: Three Rivers Press, 2007.
———. *Dreams from My Father: A Story of Race and Inheritance*. New York: Times Books, 1995.

Magazines and Newspapers

Anderton, Trish. "Obama's Jakarta Trail." *The Jakarta Post*, 22 July, 2008.

Argetsinger, Amy, and Roxanne Roberts. "The Obama Family's Multicultural Weapons." *The Washington Post*, 22 January, 2008.

Barker, Kim. "History of Schooling Distorted." *Chicago Tribune*, 25 March, 2007.

Baxter, Sarah. "White House Hopeful's 'Lost' Sister Lives in Britain." *London Times*, 5 November, 2006.

Collins, Lauren. "The Other Obama." *The New Yorker*, 10 March, 2008.

Fornek, Scott. "Auma Obama: 'Her Restlessness, Her Independence.'" *Chicago Sun-Times*, 9 September, 2007.
———. "Madelyn Payne Dunham: 'A Trailblazer.'" *Chicago Sun-Times*, 9 September, 2007.

Jones, Tim. "Barack Obama: Mother not Just a Girl from Kansas." *Chicago Tribune*, 27 March, 2007.

Kantor, Jodi. "In 2008 Race, Little Ones Go on the Trail With Daddy." *The New York Times*, 26 August 2007.

Merida, Kevin. "The Ghost of a Father." *The Washington Post*, 14 December, 2007.
———. "Oxy Remembers 'Barry' Obama '83." *Occidental College Bulletin*, 29 January, 2007.

Reyes, B. J. "Punahou Left Lasting Impression on Obama." *Honolulu Star-Bulletin*, 8 February, 2007.

Ripley, Amanda. "The Story of Barack Obama's Mother." *Time*, 9 April, 2008.

Rossi, Rosalind. "The Woman behind Obama." *Chicago Sun-Times*, 20 January, 2007.

Scharnberg, Kirsten, and Kim Barker. "The Not-So-Simple Story of Barack Obama's Youth." *Chicago Tribune*, 25 March, 2007.

Scott, Janny. "A Free-Spirited Wanderer Who Set Obama's Path." *The New York Times*, 14 March, 2008.
———. "The Story of Obama, Written by Obama." *The New York Times*, 18 May, 2008.

Slevin, Peter. "Obama Says He Regrets Land Deal With Fundraiser." *The Washington Post*, 17 December 2006.

Superville, Darlene. "Malia Obama Looks Forward to Decorating WH Room." *The Associated Press*, 7 July, 2008.

Video
"Barack Obama." A&E Biography, 2005.
Senator Obama Goes to Africa. Directed by Bob Hercules, 2007.

Internet
Official Barack Obama website
www.barackobama.com

Obama, Barack. "Keynote Address at the 2004 Democratic National Convention." Boston, MA, July 27, 2004. http://www.barackobama.com/2004/07/27/keynote_address_at_the_2004_de.php.
———. "A More Perfect Union." Speech on race in America at the National Consitution Center, Philadelphia, PA, March 18, 2008. http://my.barackobama.com/page/content/hisownwords.
———. "Senator Barack Obama's Announcement for President." Springfield, Illinois, February 10, 2007. http://www.barackobama.com/2007/02/10/remarks_of_senator_barack_obam_11.php
———. "Remarks of State Senator Barack Obama against Going to War with Iraq." Speech for an antiwar rally, Chicago, Illinois, October 2, 2002.
Barack Obama Photos: The Early Years. Chicago Tribune online. http://www.chicagotribune.com/news/politics/070323obama-early-photogallery,0,5458360.photogallery.
Interview with Maya Soetoro-Ng, Barack's sister, on YouTube. http://www.youtube.com/watch?v=7m4didWsPKE.